Mindset and Self-Talk

An Essential Guide to Transforming Negative Thinking Into Positive Thinking and Increasing Your Confidence, Self-Discipline, Success, and Productivity

© **Copyright 2019**

All Rights Reserved. No part of this book may be reproduced in any form without permission in writing from the author. Reviewers may quote brief passages in reviews.

Disclaimer: No part of this publication may be reproduced or transmitted in any form or by any means, mechanical or electronic, including photocopying or recording, or by any information storage and retrieval system, or transmitted by email without permission in writing from the publisher.

While all attempts have been made to verify the information provided in this publication, neither the author nor the publisher assumes any responsibility for errors, omissions or contrary interpretations of the subject matter herein.

This book is for entertainment purposes only. The views expressed are those of the author alone, and should not be taken as expert instruction or commands. The reader is responsible for his or her own actions.

Adherence to all applicable laws and regulations, including international, federal, state and local laws governing professional licensing, business practices, advertising and all other aspects of doing business in the US, Canada, UK or any other jurisdiction is the sole responsibility of the purchaser or reader.

Neither the author nor the publisher assumes any responsibility or liability whatsoever on the behalf of the purchaser or reader of these materials. Any perceived slight of any individual or organization is purely unintentional.

Contents

Part 1: Mindset 0

INTRODUCTION 1

CHAPTER 1 3

CHAPTER 2 13

CHAPTER 3 21

CHAPTER 4 28

CHAPTER 5 35

CHAPTER 6 43

CHAPTER 7 49

CHAPTER 8 59

CHAPTER 9 69

CHAPTER 10 81

CONCLUSION 93

INTRODUCTION 96

CHAPTER 1: WHERE DOES NEGATIVE SELF-TALK COME FROM?...................98

- THE POWER OF THOUGHT..99
- THE SUBCONSCIOUS MIND..100
- THE ORIGINS OF NEGATIVE THOUGHTS...101
- SO HOW DOES IT WORK?..104
- THE BLANK SLATE..105
- THE SELF-TALK JOURNAL..106
- WHEN SOMETHING BECOMES A PROGRAM, IT'S AN AUTOMATIC RESPONSE..................107
- THE FORMATION OF HABITS AND DESIRES...108
- EXTERNAL CIRCUMSTANCES CREATE NEGATIVE THINKING: YOU HAVE TO CHANGE IT FROM WITHIN..109
- SIMPLE WAYS TO REPROGRAM YOUR THOUGHT PROCESSES AND FEELINGS....................110
- CHANGING YOUR HABITS...110
- NEGATIVE EMOTIONS ARE NORMAL...113
- AFFIRMATIONS..113
- REPROGRAMMING THE SUBCONSCIOUS MIND..115

CHAPTER 2: WHY SELF-LOVE MATTERS..117

- HOW AND WHY NEGATIVE SELF-TALK MANIFESTS IN NEGATIVE RESULTS.....................118
- THE REALITY DISTORTION FIELD..120
- LEARNED HELPLESSNESS...125
- REFRAMING YOUR THOUGHTS..127
- ADOPT AN ATTITUDE OF BEING IN CONTROL...128
- CATEGORIZING YOUR NEGATIVE SELF-TALK...129
- TURN NEGATIVE THOUGHTS INTO POSITIVE THOUGHTS...........................130
- THE IMPORTANCE OF RAISING CHILDREN WITH A POSITIVE ATTITUDE........130

CHAPTER 3: THE LEVELS OF SELF-TALK..137

- ACCEPTANCE AND HARMFUL SELF-TALK...137
- RECOGNIZING NEGATIVE SELF-TALK AND THE NEED TO CHANGE IT...........139
- MAKING A DECISION TO CHANGE...142
- CAN-DO SELF-TALK (BETTER YOU)..146
- UNIVERSAL AFFIRMATION..147
- SUMMARY: THE FIVE LEVELS OF SELF-TALK...148

CHAPTER 4: STOP THE BLAME GAME..149

- BLAMING SOMEONE ELSE FOR YOUR PROBLEMS....................................150
- BLAMING YOURSELF..154
- MANIPULATIVE BLAME..156

CHAPTER 5: CONFRONTING NEGATIVE SELF TALK...158

- RECOGNIZING NEGATIVE SELF-TALK...158
- CATCHING YOURSELF USING NEGATIVE SELF-TALK..................................160

    Labeling Negative Self-Talk 161
    Telling Your Negative Thoughts to F-Off 161
    Changing Perspectives 163
    Replacing Negative Thoughts 164
    Getting Rid of Negative Self-Talk and Replacing it Can Change How You Feel .. 166

CHAPTER 6: FOSTERING SELF ESTEEM 168

    Stop Being Your Own Bully 168
    Recognizing Yourself as Worthy 169
    Steps to Foster Self-Love and Self-Esteem 169
    Take Up Hobbies or Volunteer 173
    Building a Foundation of Self-Esteem 174
    Becoming a Leader of Self 176

CHAPTER 7: EMOTIONAL INTELLIGENCE 178

    Awareness 178
    Regulating Your Emotions 180
    Becoming Sensitive to Emotional Signals 181
    Changing Your Emotional States 181

CHAPTER 8: STRENGTHEN THE MENTAL MUSCLE 183

    Get Tough and Have Your Own Back 183
    Remaining Strong in the Face of Adversity 185
    Tips for Maintaining a Strong Mindset and Staying Positive 185

CHAPTER 9: 500 AFFIRMATIONS FOR A POSITIVE AND OPTIMISTIC OUTLOOK 187

CONCLUSION 207

CHECK OUT ANOTHER BOOK BY MARK DUDLEY 209

Part 1: Mindset

Unlocking the Power of Positive Thinking: Skyrocketing your Confidence, Success, Self-Discipline, Productivity, Focus, Self-Esteem, Mental Toughness, Social Intelligence and Leadership Skills

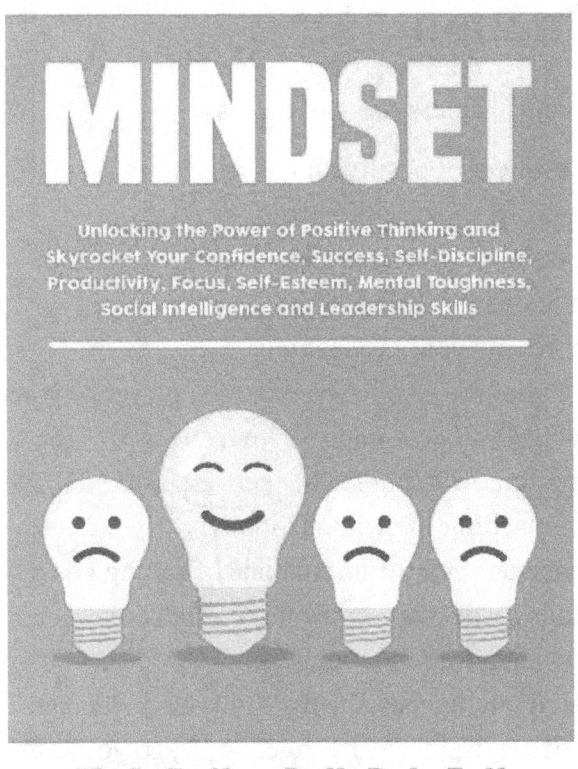

Introduction

In the following chapters, we will discuss:

- The power of positive thinking
- Boosting your confidence
- Skyrocketing your success
- Developing self-discipline
- Improving your productivity
- The importance of harnessing the power of your emotions
- Practical ways to improve your focus
- Tips on how to boost your self-esteem
- Approaching life without apology
- Understanding the importance of setting goals
- Finding ways to become more productive
- Practicing mental toughness
- Social intelligence: Using it to your advantage
- Leadership skills: Effectively manage your life
- Discovering your leadership type…and much more!

If you are struggling with accomplishing your goals, learning your destiny, and tackling life with a positive attitude, then this book is for you! Read on to learn practical ways of ensuring that your future remains bright by harnessing the power of positive thinking and activating the Law of Attraction.

There are plenty of books on this subject; we are glad you chose this one. Please enjoy!

Chapter 1

The Power of Positive Thinking

When changing your mindset, the first area to address is your thinking processes. Positive thinking helps you in each area of life; when you proactively change how your mind assesses experiences, you begin stepping into a new, better, and brighter future!

- **Living Each Day with Joy**

Each day is a new beginning. Approaching each day with a joyful attitude results in changes. Life begins to look different, bringing positivity into areas in which you have struggled. Below you will find some tips and some strategies to use so that you can approach each day with a joyful attitude and reap the benefits.

- **Don't Wait to Be Happy**

Happiness is your jurisdiction. Your attitude and outlook on life play a major role in determining happiness. If you are waiting for happiness to arrive at your doorstep, you'll be disappointed! It's up to you to *make your happiness.*

- **Seek Happiness Now**

Find something that makes you happy and *pursue it.* Go out on a limb (where the fruit is) and find the results you seek. Making the effort is part of the journey, bringing its own rewards, so resist any tendency to consider the undertaking as anything but positive. Start now!

- **Practice Self-Care**

Meditation, proper nutrition, exercise, and affirmations are examples of how you can practice self-care. Taking care of yourself is a necessary part of growth and maintaining a healthy relationship with yourself, and without it, negativity may creep into your life. Looking after your body and soul is one of the most important tasks in your life.

- **Stop Worrying**

Worrying never accomplishes anything. You cannot seek out happiness if your mind is constantly anxious. Consider journaling about your concerns; seeing them on paper may provide a different perspective, bringing both relief and solutions. Create a habit of proactivity, and you'll not only gain self-confidence, but you'll also be releasing those worries.

- **Be Grateful**

Being grateful helps you understand the good things that you have, shifting your focus away from the things that you don't have. Mindfully thinking about your good fortune increases happiness, filling your days with joy. Begin by making a list of the areas in your life for which you are thankful, listing everything big or small. Reflect on this list and watch how your attitude and perspective changes!

- **Add Positive People to Your World**

Never underestimate the power of positive people. Those we surround ourselves with matter because we pick up on their emotions (or "vibes"), allowing them to affect our energy. If you are always in the company of negative complainers, it will eventually rob you of your peace. Instead, surround yourself with a positive and upbeat crowd which helps you maintain this attitude in yourself. Your joy and happiness should take precedence over negative relationships.

- **Love and Laugh More Often**

Loving yourself becomes easier when you practice loving others. Look for opportunities for displaying affection, forgiveness, empathy, and understanding. Learn to laugh at yourself and laugh with others, increasing happiness for you both. You'll begin experiencing the lasting effects of love and laughter while increasing your positive outlook on life.

- **Create a Bucket List**

A bucket list catalogs everything you wish to accomplish in life; consider it the ultimate list of what you would like to do. For some, it might include climbing Mount Everest; for others, it may be falling in love. Remember that each goal should bring you joy! Making your bucket list a priority is another exercise in self-care because you are making *yourself a* priority, as well.

- **Plan for Happiness**

Remember: ultimately, you control your happiness, and establishing a planned pathway to create joy in your life is another priority. Figure out what brings you joy and create a plan that makes happiness and joy a mainstay in your life. Then proceed on that pathway with a joyful attitude.

Taking Responsibility for Your Present and Future

To adopt a positive mindset, you need to learn to embrace your past, your present, and your future. Taking responsibility for your actions is an effective way to change your life; it is an acknowledgment that you control what your life looks like - both now and in the future.

- **Stop the Blame Game**

Blaming someone else for what has - or has not - happened to you does nothing to help create the life that you want for yourself. Even if a person has brought you harm, releasing blame enables you to move on and embrace a more positive future for yourself.

- **Excuses Don't Help**

Stop making excuses for why you can't do something, why you aren't where you want to be, or any other negative thought. Excuses do nothing to further your goals and entertaining them only holds you back, wasting time and energy that should be spent fulfilling your purpose and achieving happiness. Instead of rationalizing, do something positive and constructive in reaching your goals.

- **Practice Self-Compassion**

Learning to be compassionate with yourself requires forgiving yourself for shortcomings, admitting your weaknesses, and understanding that you cannot do everything. Releasing control of every aspect of your life is the first step on the path towards appropriate self-compassion. You will need to work on this area if you struggle with self-love and self-kindness; success will not come if you don't believe that you deserve value and grace.

- **Accept and Use Your Negative Emotions**

Try as you may to avoid them, negative emotions are part of life. Learning to accept and harness the power of these negative emotions will boost your ability to improve yourself, leading to a happier life. You'll find that negative emotions occur less often, resulting in a more positive outlook on everything you encounter.

- **Find Happiness Internally, Not Externally**

Unhappiness is usually caused by seeking happiness externally. Looking outside yourself for happiness is a trap; find that joy within yourself and notice the change in your thinking patterns. Keeping your focus inward is a way of taking responsibility for who you are and what you do and is an important step towards maturity.

- **Keep Your Word**

Part of accepting and taking responsibility for yourself and your actions starts with keeping your word. If you say you are going to do something, then do it or plan for an alternative that keeps your promise. This is vital to accepting your past, present, and future because if you cannot keep your word, you will never accept responsibility for yourself.

- **Avoid Complaining**

Just like excuses, complaining helps nothing. Complaints take time and energy away from the critical work that you are trying to accomplish, hindering progress towards reaching your goals. We all know someone who bemoans everything in their life. Does that foster a sense of wellbeing in you? Or does it create a feeling of negativity, fueling angst or grief? Try reframing grievances into empowering statements of change. Create a life that does not include complaining!

- **Take Action**

Without taking action, how will you achieve the life that you envision? Shape your present and future by taking control, creating an action plan, and actively tackling any hurdles that stand between you and your goals.

Taking Responsibility for Your Mind and Your Body

Taking responsibility for your mind and your body involves many steps:

- <u>Sleep Well</u> – Take steps to get the right amount of sleep, making sure that the quality of your sleep is good.
- <u>Eat Well</u> – Pay attention to the food you eat, as it fuels your activity. Eating a balanced diet helps your body absorb the necessary nutrients to keep it in tip-top shape. A body fueled on junk food will not give you the results that you desire.

- Exercise - Moderate exercise is going to improve your focus, aid in improving concentration and mood, resulting in a boost of confidence.
- Be Thankful – Mindfully practice a grateful attitude. When you practice gratitude, you will find that not only does your outlook on life change, your perception of the future becomes more positive.
- Take Time to Have Fun - Everyone enjoys a good time, and studies have proven that having fun has positive effects on your life. When you take time to do activities that you enjoy, you are giving your mood a boost, as well as improving how you will tackle the future.
- Avoid Toxic People, Places, and Things - When looking to avoid negativity in your life, the best place to begin is with toxicity. Pinpoint areas in your life where negativity has a foothold, and work to eliminate the influences.
-
- Reflect and Meditate - Take the time to reflect and meditate on your life, your future, and how you plan on reaching the success you desire. If you struggle to calm your mind, find a peaceful place without distractions, and try again.

Shaping your present and your future depends on understanding and mastering each point above. You can - and will - achieve your goals, experiencing the success that you have visualized for yourself.

Tips on Self-Compassion

Self-compassion is essential to living your life with joy and for accepting responsibility for yourself. Below are tips to help you adopt a compassionate mindset.

- **Forgive Yourself**

Everyone makes mistakes, and every mistake offers a way to learn and grow. Self-forgiveness is the greatest gift you can give yourself because it allows you to move forward and shape your future. Just as we forgive others for their past mistakes, choices, or errors, we must release grudges against ourselves. This is the greatest gift, realizing that nothing can change the past, but you can shape your future.

- **Adopt a Growth Mindset**

After granting yourself forgiveness, move towards a mindset that invites and promotes personal growth in terms of your talents and skills. Develop and continue to hone these throughout your life, and you'll experience greater ease in deciding what your future holds. You will be making changes that steer your ship on a course to that future.

- **Be Generous**

Your generosity with others will not only change someone's life but the way *they view their life*. Adopting a grateful attitude is a terrific way to enhance your thinking patterns and those of people around you, setting off good "vibes" for everyone involved.

- **Practice Being Mindful**

Mindfulness means living in the moment, consciously focusing your attention on what is happening around you *as well as within you*. Being mindful of every situation enhances your capacity for compassion.

Control Your Thoughts, Control Your Life

Controlling your thoughts is going to make a huge impact on your life. Once you can control your mind, you'll begin shaping negative thoughts into positive ones.

- **Take a Breath**

When you are experiencing negative thoughts, a good first step is to stop and breathe. By allowing yourself a moment, you are going to find that the situation loses its power. Continue to take deep breaths as you regain your composure and find your footing, allowing your mind to clear and your focus to return. *Do not be afraid to take a moment and practicing deep breathing.* Match your inhaling to your exhaling; this restores calmness and inner peace.

- **Stay Present**

By remaining mindful in the present moment, you cannot fret about the past or the future. You cultivate inner peace by reducing worries, and that's the secret power of remaining present: stay focused on what you can control and release that which you cannot control.

- **Deal in Facts, Not Opinions**

Make sure to look at – and understand - the facts when facing situations where your self-esteem may be in jeopardy. Know what you are good at, understand that you are worthy of good things, and forget about the opinions of others. You may not be viewing yourself in the right light if your self-esteem is suffering. Consider taking an in-depth look at how you view yourself *in light of how others view you.* Establish your own perspective of yourself (practicing self-compassion) and stop worrying about the opinions of others.

- **Address Your Thoughts**

When you find yourself ruminating on negative things, stop and address your thoughts. This prevents your mind from spiraling out of control, allowing you to refine and reform your mindset into a more positive outlook.

- **Find a Comfortable Place**

Finding a comfortable and peaceful place to relax is key to allowing yourself to take control of your thoughts. Be sure that you can remove all distractions that may inhibit a clear, uninterrupted mind.

- **Divert Your Thoughts with Activity**

If you find your thoughts spiraling out of control, try diverting your attention. Find an activity that precludes heavy thinking: helping others, watching a movie, going to an art gallery, etc.

- **Seek Advice for Troubling Thoughts**

When troubling thoughts take over and affect your daily living, seek advice. Gaining an outside perspective often quiets the mind's storm, providing hope and the possibility of resolution.

- **Make Mental Health a Top Priority**

Make sure that you are treating mental health seriously. Relentless negative thinking generally has underlying causes that should be addressed; these thought processes may be arising from an organic imbalance that is easily treatable. Seeking help and advice is always a good idea, especially if you are deeply concerned with your thought life.

Know Your Triggers

When you find yourself dealing with negative thoughts (and the patterns seem repetitive) keep track of what you were doing before these thoughts. Mindfully tracking how and when your thoughts are being shaped will help you identify and avoid triggers. By understanding what triggers these thought patterns, you will then be able to avoid the triggers.

Meditate

Meditation is a form of clearing your mind and gaining control. Meditation can also help realign your thought processes because you are centering yourself and actively choosing to think about other matters.

Understand What You Can - and Can't - Control

By understanding what you can control, you are going to be able to let go of the stuff that you cannot control. Not everything in your life is going to be under your control! When you learn to accept that, you're going to see your thought patterns change. Control what you can and let go of the rest!

Positive thinking is going to reshape your life, and you will see results. People often underestimate the power of positive thinking but implementing this strategy in your life activates the Law of Attraction. We will discuss the Law of Attraction later on in the book but remember that powerful thinking starts by reshaping negative thoughts into positive ones.

Chapter 2

Boost Your Confidence

Your confidence plays a critical role when analyzing your mindset; it also affects the amount of success you can expect from life. By boosting your confidence, you're going to see changes in your thought processes - as well as in your life.

Gaining self-confidence shows that you are in control of your destiny as well is your life. How are some ways that you can tell that you are in control? Below are some examples of how you are in control of your life - and thriving!

If you lose your job, you will be okay. By adopting the right mindset, you will understand that losing your job is not an obstacle or an end of the world situation. Rather, you will view this as an opportunity to change. Losing your job may very well be the kick-start that you needed to start your own business, change career paths, or even move to a different city. When you control your destiny, things like losing your job are not going to send you into a tailspin, but rather they will empower you to change where you are at.

Another example: acting on your instincts in your dating life. Perhaps you are waiting for the right person (and you feel like you found that person), but he or she is unaware of your interest. When you are in control of your life, you understand that it is perfectly acceptable for you to initiate the first encounter, even if it does not feel socially acceptable. Controlling your life includes every area, including your love life. Take action, and don't wait - reach out and grab what you want.

By being in control of your own life, you understand that failure is just part of the journey, accepting them and moving on. The chance to grow as an individual is important – one reason that we face failure. How you handle the failure is going to determine whether you are controlling your life or your life is controlling you. Do not allow yourself to wallow in self-pity! Instead, take control of the situation and rectify it. You know what you want out of life, and no one else is going to give it to you. Take control of your situation and the direction your life is taking – make progress on your own terms.

Owning Who You Are

Part of taking control of your own life and your destiny includes knowing *who you are* and *owning that person*. Accept responsibility for who you are and the actions that you take, and you will see a world of difference in your life. How do you own and accept responsibility for yourself?

- **Accept That You Are a Work-in-Progress**

Each of us grows into the person we wish to be – we are all a work-in-progress! Once you accept the fact that you will not reach perfection, you will find that your perspective on life changes. Continue to learn and grow, understanding that while you may not be perfect, you are evolving into a better person each day.

Explore Who You Are

Self-awareness is a huge part of growing as an individual. Take the time to get to know yourself, understanding your weaknesses, and then learning how those weaknesses shape you as an individual. It's also important to understand what your strengths are and how you can use those to your advantage. Consider journaling to find out what you truly like and don't like, what you are good at, and areas where you may need improvement. The process of self-awareness is going to continue throughout your lifetime.

- **Let Go of What You Cannot Control**

Perhaps you are a person who needs to be in control of every area of their life. You could be experiencing frustration because life continues to throw you curveballs that you have no chance of controlling. Once you understand – then accept – that there are going to be things in your life that you cannot control, you'll find that you are happier and more capable than you first thought. This process increases your self-confidence, as you stop blaming yourself for failures that you have no control over.

- **Face Your Fears**

By facing your fears, you are going to feel better about yourself. Facing your fears does not mean that you overcome them; it means that you understand that you *can continue* even though you are afraid. Pushing through that fear and moving beyond it is an important step towards success.

- **Quiet Your Inner Critic**

Each of us has thoughts running through our heads, seeding doubt that we are not good enough, what we did was stupid, or that we'll never succeed. Thoughts like that come from your inner critic, and you need to learn to silence that voice! Clearly, self-confidence increases when you quit listening to that voice; you will accomplish more, feeling more confident in each task that you take on.

- **Experience Your Emotions, Good or Bad**

We all experience emotions daily. The good emotions seem acceptable, but the bad emotions tend to bring shame. Once you learn to accept that "bad" emotions are okay, you're going to feel better about yourself. Stop attaching negative thoughts to negative emotions! Remember that negative emotions can be driving you to succeed, so embrace the good and the bad.

- **Share Your Vulnerability**

Becoming vulnerable to someone is a huge step. While it may feel like vulnerability is a weakness, it can be viewed as a positive trait. Becoming vulnerable to another individual shows a level of trust – and trust is a critical part of growth. Vulnerability is also important because showing it also reaffirms that you are worthy; this can do wonders for your self-confidence!

- **Find Out How Others View You**

This is a tricky area. While seeking approval from others should never be a high priority, your self-awareness depends partially on sensing how others see you. What do they see as your strengths and your weaknesses? Find out how others view you, taking the feedback as an opportunity to improve, reshaping some weaknesses, and making them into strengths. Never take the opinions of others as fact, but compare how they see you to how you see yourself.

- **Look at the Best Parts of You**

Remember to be proud of aspects of yourself that you like! If you've taken up journaling, make a list of your characteristics or accomplishments that make you feel successful. Write down your strengths and make a point to focus on this at least once a day. These daily affirmations will go a long way in building your self-confidence and reminding you that you are worthy of self-praise.

Make Your Destiny – Plan Your Ideal Future

You must understand that you are in control of your destiny and that you can *(and should)* shape your future. Once you embrace this truth, you'll see that your choices take on new importance.

This can become an exciting part of self-growth! Take the time to develop a vision for your future and then plan for that future. Write down your dreams and what you hope to accomplish. Dream big, understanding that you can do whatever you set your mind to and no one can hold you back. If you accept the power within to form your future, you can map it out, and run with it!

- **Be Realistic**

Realism and practicality do play a part in your future, and limitations do exist. That said, don't allow yourself to dwell on what you can't do though. Instead, apply realistic thinking, consider appropriate timeframes for reaching your goals. For example, it may be fun to consider losing 100 pounds in 30 days, but it's also unrealistic (and dangerous!) Give yourself a break – be realistic!

- **Understanding Your Passion**

While moving towards the goal line, remind yourself *who you are working for!* Whose goals are you trying to reach: your own, or someone else's? Don't lose focus on your own goals and the skills it takes to reach them. While you may be doing someone else's work for them, remind yourself daily about your future goals and how your daily life moves you closer to reaching them. Your passion fuels your daily work, and your daily work is moving you closer to reaching your goals. If you find that you are moving through days without passion, stop to consider where your focus lies: yourself or others?

- **Honesty**

Be honest with yourself about what you can accomplish. Do you have the drive that it takes and have you developed the passion that you need to succeed? Honestly look at what you are good at, what you are passionate about, and how all of these can play a part in your future. Often, we overlook our passion when considering our future, forgetting that a passionless life drains confidence. The world tells us we must march along, working only for others, and leaving our future in their hands, not our own! Apply honesty regarding your skills and goals, but remember that passion should be fueling your travels, not solely necessity or other people's goals.

- **Consider Your Tools and Resources**

When shaping your destiny and taking control of your life, you must assess the tools and resources available to take you to your desired future. What skills do you have readily available? Are you actively honing those skills in anticipation of the day that you get to reach out and take control? Again, making a list will help you scrutinize those abilities, tools, and resources as you make your way in life.

- **Ignore the Critics**

You will face critics throughout your life; there will always be someone saying you cannot do something. Remember that others' opinions are just that: opinions. Hearing critical voices is different than *listening to them!* Often critics have met with failure in their own lives, and they are just projecting that failure onto your life. Don't give them the power to tear down your self-confidence!

- **Settle for Nothing Less than Excellence**

Settling for mediocrity leads you down a dead-end path. Striving for excellence, reshaping your thought processes, understanding that you are worthy of a bright future; that mindset takes you to success. Affirm your self-worth daily, remembering that you do not deserve mere adequacy – you deserve excellence!

Tips to Boost Your Confidence

This chapter has been all about your self-confidence and how it's going to help you be in control of your life and take control of your destiny. What if you don't feel great about yourself? How do you go about boosting your self-confidence and loving who you are?

Choose to Accept You

If you do not accept to you are, then others sense that, making it difficult for them to accept you. Learning to love yourself is the first step in boosting your self-confidence! Remember to quell the critics; just because somebody else thinks something is wrong with you *does not make them right*. Embrace your quirks and your idiosyncrasies and love yourself despite what anyone else tells you. While you may be a work-in-progress, you are moving towards perfection. In the interim, be humble where you may lack luster, and take advantage of your naturally good characteristics to shine!

Perfectionism – a Fallacy

Do not fall for the false assumption that you need to be – or can be – perfect. Understanding that simple concept frees you to accept that how you are - right now - is good enough. Embracing this idea allows you to be happier with yourself. This does not mean that you ignore weaknesses, limitations, or faults; being aware of these is the only way to begin overcoming them. We cannot change what we do not know. That said, letting go of perfectionism boosts your self-confidence, enabling you to embrace everything about what makes you unique.

Understand the Confidence Within

Have you ever felt the glimmer of confidence in something that you have done utterly well? Do you allow that small flame to engulf every part of who you are, or do you extinguish that flame? Perhaps you've had confidence within you but felt that it was somehow wrong to embrace it. Find the confidence within you and allow that light to shine! There is greatness within you – it should be received enthusiastically. Dig deep and discover the confidence you already have and watch your life change for the better.

- **Ignore Your Inner Critic**

Earlier in the chapter, we discussed quieting your inner critic – no one needs to have a constant negative voice telling them they are not good enough. We are our own worst critic. No one else is going to be as hard on you as you are on yourself, and you need to stop this pattern. Understanding that you can reshape your thoughts and quiet the critic will send your confidence soaring. If we have outside negative voices attacking us every day, do we need to add our voice to the mix? Consider that question. If you are listening to the outside, taking to heart every bad comment, your inner voice and inner thoughts will mirror that sentiment. Calm and ignore your inner critic. Nothing beneficial is going to come from you criticizing yourself. Simply put: love yourself enough to close your ears to negativity within.

Ask for Help

Perhaps you don't know - or cannot accept – that you are worthy. Do not feel afraid to ask for help from someone that you trust (a friend or a professional.) Sometimes we need to have another person validate what we are feeling. Find someone that you trust and that you can be honest with to help you sort through who you are.

Dwell on the Positive, Not the Negative

Focus on the positive and forget the negative. That is easier said than done, but it is something that you need to strive for. When you concentrate on looking for positives, that's what you begin to see all around you (and it works with negatives, as well!) Optimism is a great trait to embrace as it leads to a happier and more successful life. It is your choice, take control and mindfully choose to dwell on the positive aspects of every day, making a mental note of them as you fall asleep. Those obstacles that you faced on your way to a promotion? No problem! Those were just road signs to improvement. Choosing how you view everything that happens puts you in control of your confidence – or lack of confidence.

Your confidence is an essential part of who you are, and in the face of a world of negativity, your success depends on your ability to understand the correlation between confidence and success in life. You are in control of your destiny; your life does not control you. Take time to work on your self-confidence if you struggle in this area. You are worthy, and you are important. Never forget that you deserve happiness and greatness.

Chapter 3

Success and You

Most people want to be successful in life, and I imagine you are one of those people. You picked up this book, didn't you? This shows you are willing to put the work in to make yourself successful. Success depends on many factors: how you approach the obstacles in life, how you live life, and how you tackle problems – all these determine the level of success that you experience.

Live Life on Your Terms

You do not need the validation of someone else to feel important or to feel worthy of success. Learning to live life on your terms is a huge step and will not only allow you to experience success, but it will also allow you to do what you want and what you love without the validation of someone else.

- **Dream A Little or A Lot**

Your dreams are important, and they are a vital part of your success. Give yourself a chance to dream and embrace the life that you want. Let your mind wander, journal about your dreams, and set out to make them a reality. Dreaming is not only allowed, but it is also encouraged! Our dreams determine what we need to be doing in life; without them, we flounder.

- **Consider Your Reality**

Take a moment and understand where you are at in your life. Take stock of your reality now and taking steps to better yourself becomes your path into the life you've envisioned for yourself. What changes do you need to make to help you achieve your goals? How do you need to approach life so that you can reach where you want to be? Understanding where you are at in life, what you want, and how to get there is important.

- **Think, but Don't Dwell, About the Past**

What choices have you made in the past that have either advanced where you want to be or hindered your progress? Take some time to think about where you have been so that you can take steps to get where you want to be. Your past does not define you, but learning from obstacles you've faced is an important part of living life on your terms and shaping your life into what you want it to be. Do not allow yourself to criticize your past, but objectively ponder where you have been.

- **Check Your Options**

Understand the options that are available to you. By doing this, you are going to know where you can go in life and how to get there. Perhaps you need to make some changes at the moment to get you where you need to go. If you desire to live in Paris, but your bank account is empty, perhaps you need to make some money and learn some skills to keep you afloat once you get to Paris. Understanding the options that are available to you is important so that you can take steps to get you where you desire.

- **Seek Advice**

Advice is important only if it comes from somebody that you trust. Listening to those who truly do not have your best interests at heart is dangerous; they may seek to tear you down rather than build you up. A trusted friend or professional is likely to provide constructive feedback, helping you reach your goals. Seek advice from somebody who has already achieved what you are trying to achieve and who can help you understand the process. Understanding how they got to where you want to be is beneficial so that you can mimic their success. The steps that they have taken are going to give you guidelines and help you avoid common pitfalls.

- **Make a Plan**

For some people, planning is fun – others despise it! Having a plan is a good idea when you are looking to make your life what you wanted to be. When you have a plan, you are going to know if you are on the right path. Without a plan, you could end up thinking you're on the right path, but then fail to succeed.

- **Take Action**

Nothing happens without effort, and that includes achieving your goals. To live life on your terms and achieve the goals that you have set for yourself, you must act. Once you've made a plan, set out to make that plan a reality. The effort that you put into your goals and the journey that you take is often as (or more) important than the result. Have confidence that you are going to succeed, but if you miss the mark, take action to correct where you went wrong.

- **Law of Attraction**

The Law of Attraction states that the power of the universe is going to help you manifest the life that you want. In applies to thoughts, ideas, people, situations, and circumstances. The Law of Attraction allows you to manifest whatever it is you desire.

Goal Setting

Your goals are important, and you need to set goals for your life. Once you have set your goals, you have a plan to get the life that you want. Remember that your goals should motivate you; if they fail to inspire you to action, consider taking another look! A side note on motivation: sometimes you need to get started to *feel that motivation!*

- **Your Goals Should Be Smart**

Smart means specific, measurable, attainable, relevant, and timely. Each of your goals should meet these requirements and if they don't, reframe them so that they do. When you follow these smart guidelines, you increase the chances of meeting your goals.

- **Write Them Down**

Write down your goals and keep that list in a place you can see them daily (refrigerator, car dash, work desk.) Keeping the list within visual range is important, helping you remember what you are doing and what you are working for. Be sure to express them with positive wording and use a to-do list to accomplish the steps that you need to take to be successful.

- **Take Action**

You've probably noticed that "take action" is a recurrent theme throughout this book. Goals without action or effort are useless. If you need to, break them down into smaller steps and use the steps to show you when you are on the right track. The steps are merely guidelines that are going to allow you to track your progress. Put effort into your goals; that effort will never be wasted.

- **Don't Give Up**

No matter what life throws you, never give up on your goals. The only way that you can fail is if you concede defeat. Your goals should be important enough to you that no matter what you face, you will not give up. Cling to the idea that quitting is not an option because your life is within your control and you will do whatever is needed to be successful.

Face Your Fears – Know They are Normal.

Your fears can become an obstacle to starting your climb to success and can be a powerful enemy – or a powerful motivator. As a natural part of life, fear can present a challenge that you meet, an enemy you can beat. Don't allow yourself to get caught up in cycles of fear. Face fears, identify the culprit and work through the experience. Remember that we all face fears; what you do with them defines courage. Allow yourself to become paralyzed into inaction, and fear wins. Acting bravely and moving forward is for winners!

- **Obstacles? No, Opportunities!**

Reframe your thought processes to view obstacles as reasons to grow rather than reasons to stop. A good way to view obstacles is to look at them as a yield sign in life. A yield sign means that you need to slow down and look around you. Once you get a picture of the environment around you, are free to go or make it changes as necessary. Obstacles do not mean that you need to stop altogether or that you are on the wrong path; they are just simple ways for you to change direction or grow as an individual.

- **Negative Feedback Is a Suggestion**

Negative feedback is important to show you ways that you need to improve. Sometimes the feedback is hard to hear, but when you train yourself to look at it as a suggestion, you will have an easier time with it. When you hear negative feedback, listen to the message, and look for ways to improve. Feel free to offer your feedback to whoever is speaking to you, helping them understand that reframing what they have to say may be important, as well.

- **Commit to Improving**

Improvement should always be your goal. This is a lifelong goal that deserves a positive commitment to success!

- **Set Small Goals**

Small goals are going to make success easier – they are the equivalent of taking baby steps. If you have large goals, break them down into smaller, more manageable steps. Track your progress so that you can look back and see how far you've come.

- **Be Accountable**

An accountability partner is a good option because when you have someone who is monitoring your progress with you, you are less likely to let them down. Another way to be held accountable is to let others know the goals that you have for yourself. Once you've made your goals known to others, you've created one more element of motivation in terms of reaching those goals.

- **Motivate Yourself**

The funny thing about motivation is that sometimes you need to get going to feel motivated. Take the first step and get yourself psyched up about the goals that you're trying to achieve. By doing this, you're going to see what you are capable of and you can keep yourself motivated by seeing the progress that you're making.

- **Keep Going, Despite Setbacks**

Setbacks are bound to happen, and if you have a plan of how to handle them, you're going to be able to keep going and maintain your progress. Don't let a setback stop you! Instead, take a moment, discover the cause, and change direction as needed. Remember that the only true failure is quitting.

Successful Relationships

To be successful in life, you need to understand how relationships work and how to hone your "people skills." Perhaps you're not a people person; you still need to learn what makes relationships successful and how to have positive interactions with people. When you improve those important skills, you'll find that your relationships are richer and more rewarding.

• What Are Your Relationship Needs?

Make sure to identify your own needs in a relationship. Yes, the needs of the other person are important, but your needs are important as well. If you are not getting what you need out of a relationship, let the other person know, and be willing to let the relationship end.

• Make Time to Build Relationships

Sometimes life gets busy. It takes time and effort to build and maintain relationships, and if you aren't able or willing to nurture them, they die on the vine. Always look for ways to build new relationships, because the connections that you have with other individuals are going to play a vital role in how you view yourself - and your success. Keep in mind that everyone enjoys feeling valued, appreciated, and cared for, but they'll never know if you don't take the time and effort to show it! Find creative ways to show that you are keeping up with their life, that their accomplishments matter, and that they play a significant role in your life.

• Maintain a Positive Attitude

You'll hear this a lot in this book, as well: build and maintain an adventurous, ambitious, and positive attitude! Your relationships will thrive because no one likes to hang around with a downer.

• Set Boundaries

While positive relationships are important, you must set boundaries for those around you, letting them know what you are willing to do, when you are available, what you will tolerate, and what you expect from them. This goes for work and personal relationships. Otherwise, your time and energy are not being preserved.

Chapter 4

Improve Your Self-Discipline

A combination of focus and self-discipline is the grease that keeps the success-engine running smoothly. Both are skills you should develop and strengthen.

Tips for Self-Discipline

Self-discipline is a powerful tool in achieving success and reaching your goals. A critical by-product is finding that your determination has deepened, and your motivation is fueled. Here are some tips to improve your self-discipline.

- **Acknowledge Your Weaknesses**

While we all have weaknesses, those who acknowledge them have taken the first step towards improving their self-discipline. You cannot change what you don't see; failing to bring light to your weaknesses is a sure hindrance on your path to success. Once you've identified weaknesses, remember to commit to taking consistent action to improve those areas of your life.

- **Avoid Temptations**

Once you've identified your weaknesses, look for patterns (or triggers) that launch the temptation to succumb to that shortcoming.

Again – if you can't see it, you can't stop it! By determining the exact provocation or trigger, you may begin to see these temptations differently. Given a chance to avoid them altogether, you will see your self-discipline and willpower increase. Don't forget: mindfully creating a list of weaknesses and triggers for temptation (and placing them in view) will help avoid situations that challenge your willpower.

- **Have Clear Expectations**

Know what you expect and what you must do to achieve your goals. If you are unsure of your expectations, how can you know when they've been fulfilled? Take time to clearly identify what you are trying to achieve as well as how you plan on getting to that destination?

- **Practice Self-Discipline - It Doesn't Come Naturally**

No one is born with self-discipline; like a muscle, it must be exercised! When you see others reaching their goals through self-mastery, remember that this was their decision, not a magical destiny. Knowing it requires efforts from us all may be key to helping you remain steadfast in reaching your goals.

- **Create Positive Habits**

Be mindful (starting today) of your habits, the routines that you follow, and the patterns that are part of your life. Determine which habits move you towards your goals, and which move you away from your goals. Make a plan to eliminate the unhelpful habits, and an equally strong plan to incorporate positive habits into your routine, making them a part of who you are.

- **Nutrition Is Important**

This one is simple: It's hard to maintain self-discipline when your body is feeble; nutrition is key to feeling your strongest and best. Make proper nutrition a priority in your life!

- **Willpower May Not Be What You Think**

Willpower is your ability to avoid temptations and triggers, doing what you know is crucial to your success – even when you don't feel like it. What is your idea of willpower? Perhaps you have misconceptions about willpower and self-discipline; take a closer look to see if you are seeing these traits in the best light possible.

- **Have A Plan B**

There will be times your willpower or self-discipline is weak. Having a backup plan provides a way back to the path when you are temporarily lost – before your plan goes over the cliff entirely! Give yourself a chance to rectify the situation, allowing yourself grace, forgiveness, and an opportunity to try again without starting a square one again.

- **Reward progress**

Keep track of the progress that you are making and reward yourself when your willpower shines. Soon the rewards become bonuses rather than motivation. When you track the progress that you are making, you can see for yourself exactly what you have accomplished. It's easy to forget the progress that you have made, and by visually registering your forward track, you self-validate and enhance your capacity for self-discipline.

- **Forgive and Move On, Be Kind to Yourself**

Everyone needs forgiveness at some point in their life. Often, we are harder on ourselves than others, withholding forgiveness for silly reasons. Perhaps you feel that if you punish yourself for slipping and making a mistake, you'll move faster towards your goals later. This is a myth, and you are more likely to improve yourself if you offer forgiveness rather than punishment. Remember to practice self-compassion as you move towards improving yourself!

Tips for Focus

Maintaining focus on our path and goal is an essential element to success, but too often an element we fail to master. Improving your focus keeps you on task, ensuring that you accomplish everything you set out to accomplish in life. Here are some tips to help you build and improve your focus.

- **Exercise**

Regular exercise frees your mind of the clutter life sends your way, helping you focus better. Decluttering one's thoughts and keeping one's body healthy are essential traits of a person who is determined to reach their goals.

- **Stay Hydrated**

Along with exercise and proper nutrition, it's important to remember to stay hydrated. Drinking enough water helps your brain function better. Besides, if you are dehydrated, you'll be distracted with what your body needs and not the task at hand. It's better to avoid the distraction by making sure that you get the proper amount of water for your body.

- **Look at What Is Important in Life**

What's important to you in life is going may look very different than what's important to someone else. Make sure that you identify what is important to you and focus on that. Everything else is either a distraction or a benefit, but your focus should remain on what you value. By focusing on what you value most, you are allowing yourself to let go of the distractions, which will improve your focus.

- **Avoid Distractions**

Distractions are everywhere in life, and you are probably already aware of those that grab your attention the most. Perhaps you are distracted by your phone. If this is the case, then you need to make sure that you put your phone away when you have important tasks to accomplish. Leave it across the room, hide it in a drawer - do whatever you need to ensure that you are going to be able to stay on task. Keep a list of what distracts you, and before you begin working, take some time to put those distractions away. When you regularly do this, you are going to see an improvement in your focus.

- **Stop Multitasking**

Multitasking is a horrible idea. Multitasking accomplishes nothing other than spreading your focus thinly over several projects. None of the projects are going to get accomplished with great detail because you're not giving each one the full attention it deserves. Make it a habit to focus on one task or activity at a time; you'll soon discover your ability to complete the objective much faster and better.

- **Small Steps**

Rome was not built in a day, and neither is your focus going to be improved in one sitting. Set small goals and take small steps that are going to help you in the long run. Each small advancement is an accomplishment, and you should be proud of it. Do not expect gigantic leaps, but rather focus on the small steps in progress that you're making. When you are worrying about making large advancements, your focus is going to be off. Become used to taking small steps, and leave the big ones for giants.

- **Refocus as Needed**

When you lose focus, take a moment, and breathe. From there, refocus and get back to work. Do not berate yourself; distraction is a human condition. Acknowledge your humanness, refocus, and move on.

Tips for Meditation

Meditation is an effective way to build your concentration and focus. A lovely by-product is a reduction in stress levels! Below you'll find some tips for meditation.

- **Designated Space**

Have a space reserved solely for your meditation time. This area should remain free of distractions and negative energy. By reserving this special area, your body will learn that when you are there, your mind is free, and your inner being is ready. In time, you will begin to crave your designated space and meditation time.

- **Make Time**

Setting aside time for this special, positive habit is an important step towards re-energizing your spirit within, improving your overall health, focus, and concentration. Clear a spot in your schedule and make this a routine every day (if possible). Just after waking and just before bedtime are both good times to practice meditation, as you are most relaxed and better able to lose yourself in meditation.

- **Start a Routine**

Routines involve structuring your day in such a way that you avoid unnecessary decisions, preparing your body prepared for the needed work. When you are on autopilot, you will find that simple tasks are easier and simple decisions do not take extra thought. When you start a routine that involves meditation, you find that your body is programmed to anticipate this activity – and you feel more prepared. Your body is going to start to relax before the anticipated meditation time, and this allows your mind to wander fully.

- **Get Comfortable**

Change comfortable and non-restricting clothes, giving your body the chance to relax and experience the full benefits of meditation. Sit in a comfortable position, perhaps using pillows or mats to soften the effects of a hard surface. That said, don't get *too* comfortable or you may fall asleep!

- **Breathe**

As you begin your meditative state, pay attention to your breathing. Breathe in through your nose and exhale through your mouth. Make sure that the inhale lasts as long as the exhale. Keep a rhythm to your breathing, and breathe deeply. Breathing is an important part of meditating, and it allows your body to relax.

- **Let Your Mind Wander**

As you are breathing and you are feeling your body relax, let your mind wander. Do not allow yourself to stop the flow of thoughts but embrace each one that comes your way. Allowing your mind to wander reduces inhibitions, allowing your body to relax further, releasing your need to control other parts of your life at this important time of recharging.

Meditation is great to help you improve your discipline and your focus. Giving yourself the time and space to meditate (releasing control) actually improves your ability to maintain control during the parts of the day that require your utmost attention.

Further Reading Suggestions:

The Miracle of Mindfulness: An Introduction to the Practice of Meditation

By: Thich Nat Hahn

How to Meditate: A Practical Guide

By: Kathleen MacDonald

The Myth of Freedom and The Way of Meditation

By: Chugiak Trongsa

Chapter 5

Productivity

You have your goals set, you have your mindset in positive mode, but now you need actually to get to work. How in the world do you keep yourself productive when it feels like you have too much to do, but not enough time to accomplish these tasks? Productivity is important to achieve your goals, and below, you will find tips, techniques, and strategies to help increase productivity in your life.

Beat Procrastination and Embrace Productivity

Procrastinating is the enemy. At all costs, you need to avoid procrastination so that you can embrace productivity and increase your positive outcomes.

- **Breakdown Your Work into Smaller Steps**

A common theme with mindset, productivity, and achieving success in life is *small steps*. Baby steps are important to achieving your goals because when you take on too much, you run the risk of becoming overwhelmed. By becoming overwhelmed, you run the risk of giving up, leading to failure. Small steps allow you to tackle your goals and projects without feeling overwhelmed. Do not underestimate how quickly small steps add up because if you do, you are going to miss beautiful parts of the journey.

- **Be Mindful of Your Work Environment**

Your productivity is affected by the environment that you're working in. Clutter, color, air quality, and temperature can all affect your productivity. Pay attention to how cluttered your workstation is, because clutter tells your brain that more work needs to be done, and you will never fully focus on the task before you. Color can affect not only your mood but your productivity as well. Boring colors (such as browns and whites) are going to make you feel sluggish and tired. Bright or bold colors may cause your mind to race rather than focus. Air quality and temperature are important as well; when these are inadequate, you become focused on your physical comfort rather than the work ahead of you. Take some time to adjust your surroundings to optimize your productivity.

- **Set Detailed Timelines**

Sometimes we like to be vague in the deadlines that we set because we feel like we can get more accomplished if we are not pinned down by a specific timeline. Don't fall into this trap, because when you set detailed timelines and expectations, you are going to be more productive overall. Your timelines should include deadlines for each step of your task, project, or activity. Ensure that you are staying focused and on time by keeping these timelines within easy reach (within sight is even better!)

- **Identify Triggers for Procrastination**

You know what triggers you to procrastinate, and when you are honest with yourself and identify these triggers if you are going to see your productivity increase. Falling victim to these triggers only hurts yourself. Make and keep a list of known procrastination triggers, trying to avoid them when you need to be productive. Some examples of triggers could be your phone ringing, notifications being sent on your phone, or others dropping by unexpectedly. Make a decision and a choice to keep yourself away from these triggers and placing value on reaching your goals. Productivity is a skill, and you need to strengthen and hone it just like other skills.

- **Surround Yourself with Productive People**

The people you surround yourself with *do affect* your productivity. One example might be your spouse working at home with you; you may feel the need to catch up and chat often. Make a point of isolating yourself from people who distract you. By surrounding yourself with productive people who are busily pursuing their own goals, you are ensuring that you are setting yourself up for success rather than failure. Mimic the productive efforts of others around you, ingraining their good habits into your daily routine.

- **Broadcast Your Goals**

Your goals are important to you, and you should let others know about them. Broadcasting your goals is a way of having others hold you accountable, driving you to be productive and reach your goals. Sometimes just not wanting to disappoint others is a good way to increase your productivity.

- **Seek Advice**

Helpful and constructive advice is something that you should always seek. By looking for help, you are giving yourself a chance to learn new techniques and strategies that are going to help you achieve your desired results.

- **Don't Over Complicate Things**

Are you a person who somehow makes the simplest task complicated? Creating impediments kills motivation and productivity! Keep everything as simple as you can and see how much more successful you are. By over-complicating things, you are giving yourself an excuse to quit. Remember, we discussed that you need to get rid of excuses to be successful. Simple and effective is the way to go; you'll see your success skyrocket because your productivity increases.

- **Pick A Point and Start**

The most important part of any journey is the beginning. But where to start? If you have written down where you are, where you need to be, and how to get there – then start where you are and take the first step towards getting to Point B. Perhaps you need to sign up for an online class, buy a how-to book, or call a successful mentor and ask for help. Get started, or you will achieve nothing. If you are nervous about starting, you may be fearful of failure. If so, identify the fear, and commit to moving beyond it. Maybe you don't start because you fear an imperfect result. In this case, your starting point is ridding yourself of the perfection myth! Pick a spot and begin, remembering that without a start, the only ending is failure.

Productivity Tips and Techniques

Everyone can use a hand when it comes to learning new ways to be effective. Below you will find tips and techniques that are going to help you skyrocket your productivity and achieve the success that you want.

- **Don't Multitask**

Multitasking should no longer be a part of your vocabulary and shall no longer be part of your work patterns. Multitasking requires you to tackle more than one project or activity at a time. This results in a poor quality of work, less productivity, and loss of focus. If you want to increase your productivity, learn how to hyper-focus on one task at a time. See how much more you get accomplished when you are not spreading your focus across multiple tasks.

- **Take A Break**

Everyone needs a break when they're working on something. When you try to push through without breaks, you're harming your productivity. Think about a task that you do and then think about the times that you pause and daydream. Are you accomplishing anything, or are you just wasting time? These are important patterns to notice because essentially, you are taking a break, but they are not productive breaks. A productive break allows you to recharge your battery and maintain your focus. Take a walk, stretch, or get something to drink. Remember that breaks do not decrease productivity, but they increase it.

- **Small Goals Are Best**

This is another one of those common themes throughout this book! Large goals are beautiful to look at, and the big picture is amazing. However, completing large goals is complicated. Remember we said that it's best not to set complicated expectations because when you do this, you run the risk of giving up before you even begin. Break each large goal into smaller goals and monitor your progress this way. Small steps allow you to get more accomplished.

- **Use Your Most Productive Time for Important Tasks**

Each of us has time during the day that we are more productive. Pinpointing and using that time to your advantage is important. Some people work better in the mornings, accomplishing more in a few early hours than the whole afternoon. Others prefer afternoons or even late-night hours. Then there are the night owls who get more done while others are sleeping! Listening to your body and your biological clock is going to allow you to utilize the time of day that works best for you.

Reorganize Your Life and Work

To be productive, it's important to revitalize your workspace and make organization a priority. To be successful and productive, make appropriate use of the space that you have available. Below you will find some tips to reorganize your working life and increase productivity.

- **Organize Your Time**

Organizing your time is going to revitalize how you approach life. By knowing what you must do and when you have to do it, you're giving yourself a structured routine which - in the end - frees up your time. Block off the amount of time that tasks are going to take and only work on those tasks during that timeframe. It's important to schedule everything; when you have something written in your schedule, you are more likely to finish.

- **Enforce Time Limits on Work**

Remember the old proverb: "All work and no play makes Jack a dull boy." When you are only focused on working, you're going to burn yourself out, decreasing productivity. Allow time away from work to help you maintain a clear mind and motivation to succeed. If you end up running over your timeframe for working, make it a point to find time elsewhere in your schedule to have time set aside for yourself.

- **Maintain a Work Environment**

Take the appropriate measures to ensure that your environment is designated as an *only-work* environment. Don't allow yourself to intertwine tasks or activities into space. Like meditation, keeping an environment solely for working is a way of programming your body and your mind to understand that the space is specific to a specific task. This is an effective way to separate your mind away from work if you happen to work from home. Your office space should be separate from your other space. This increases your productivity because you do not feel distracted by the other stuff that could be going on instead.

- **Set Times to Check Emails and Phone Calls**

Have designated times -twice daily - to check your emails and return phone calls. If you're constantly checking your emails, this is a distraction and decreases your productivity. Phone calls also tend to be a distraction, as well. If you can, avoid taking phone calls and instead return them at the time you designate. Increasing your productivity requires that you stay on task and you avoid distractions.

- **Keep a To-Do List**

To-do lists often get bad reputations, but they are appropriate and useful, reminding you of what you need to accomplish. Keep a running list, but only designate five priorities for each day; more than five may run the risk of spreading yourself too thin or becoming distracted by other tasks that needing your attention. If five priorities are too much, consider breaking that down to three.

- **Check Your Mindset**

Maintaining a positive mindset is so important; losing that confident outlook can prevent you from being productive. Negativity should have no place in the new life that you are trying to build. If you find yourself losing momentum – examine your current mindset. Are you suffering from negative thought processes, or perhaps you received some negative feedback, and now you are questioning everything that you have accomplished? Take time each day to make sure that your mindset is appropriate and that you are looking at things optimistically. Remember, perfection is a myth, being productive is not!

- **Affirmations**

Affirmations are positive statements that you repeat to yourself daily. The statements invoke the Law of Attraction, allowing you to manifest positivity into your life. Affirmations should be spoken in the morning, and you need to make sure that you believe them! Embrace the power in telling yourself that positivity shall prevail and remind yourself that you can take action as well. Coincidences have no place in your life; what happens to you happens for a reason.

- **Visualize Your and Result**

Visualization is an effective way to increase your productivity and change your mindset. By visualizing the result that you desire, you can then implement any needed changes to your routine. Visualize your result and experience the emotions that come along with it. This makes the vision feel real, increasing the likelihood of your desired outcome.

- **Manage Your Paperwork**

Getting a strong hold on paperwork can be a challenge and maintaining that stronghold can be even harder! Allowing paperwork to accumulate and clutter your work area reduces productivity. The same applies to emails. Below are some tips to help you keep your paperwork organized and eliminate the clutter and stress associated with it.

- Regularly purge unnecessary paperwork
- Use a color-coded system
- Have a mail station
- Use labels
- Categorize
- Organize other office items

Your productivity is affected by numerous factors, but by exercising care in your environment, your health, and your mindset will put you on a path to success!

Chapter 6

Focus

During this chapter, we are going to delve further into your focus and concentration. Focus is vital to success, and you must understand how to concentrate. Dividing your attention between too many tasks is a hurdle you can avoid. In this chapter, we will discuss ways to improve her concentration and focus, the benefits of reading more, and some practical exercises which help eliminate distractions and improve your focus.

Improve Your Concentration and Focus

There are several effective tips and strategies to adopt when you are trying to improve your focus and concentration. Try a mixture of techniques, using what works best for you.

- **Rest**

Rest is vital to each area of your life. By making sure that you have enough rest, you are setting yourself up to be successful and achieve your goals; this goes for your mindset, as well. If you are not tired or sluggish, your focus and your concentration suffer, finding that maintaining a positive mindset is difficult. Make sure that you are going to bed at a reasonable time, and that you are sticking with a schedule in terms of when you get awaken each day. Keeping the routine is going to ensure that your body knows when it's time to rest. Avoiding caffeine too late in the day is another good way to make sure that your body rests when it is time to retire at night.

- **Have a Plan**

Plans are important, contributing to your concentration and focus, assisting you in understanding how to tackle any problems that come your way. Include plans to ensure that your workplace is free of distractions which can lead to wasted time and energy.

- **Control Your Diet**

Diet and exercise are important. Proper nutrition is part of improving focus and concentration. Vitamins and supplements have been shown to increase concentration, and you can also ask your physician which steps may help with focus. Supplements such as fish oil and omega-3 have been proven to increase your attention span; there are special supplements for individuals who have ADHD and ADD.

- **Mix Up Your Work Environment**

Where you physically do your work influences concentration, as mentioned in chapter five. Take time to look around your workplace with an eye for eliminating distractions, keeping temperatures comfortable, considering lighting (Is it too bright? Too dim?) Incorporating nature light improves your mood and helps with productivity. Take some time to look around your work environment – make changes that improve how you feel in your own workspace. Perhaps what worked yesterday isn't going to work a week from now, and that's okay. Just take the time to understand how your environment is affecting your focus.

- **Practice**

While it may sound silly to suggest that you should practice your focus and concentration, this is how you improve it. How do bodybuilders get their muscle and strength? They take steps to train their bodies. You can practice focus while meditating. Take time each day to practice controlling your thoughts and redirecting where your thoughts take you. This is a good way to practice focusing and concentration because you are willing yourself to follow a regimented plan. Incorporate time into your daily routine for practicing focus; soon, your body and mind will understand when it's time to focus and when it's okay to let your thoughts wander.

- **Read More, Watch Less**

Reading will enhance your ability to focus and concentrate. Screen time, such as your phone, tablet, computer, and television, disrupts your cognitive functions. Find books that you enjoy and start turning pages; the benefits of reading are amazing.

- **Mental Stimulation**

Reading stimulates your mind. When watching television, you are focusing on the screen – not working your brain. It's important to stimulate your mind because, without it, you're going to lose skills valuable and vital skills such as problem-solving and vocabulary. Your memory will fade faster without mental stimulation.

- **Reduces Stress**

Reading is a great way to reduce stress. Allowing yourself to be lost in a book is a good way to forget about the problems plaguing you.

- **Gain Knowledge**

Books are written each day on every subject imaginable. If you're not a person who enjoys fiction, nonfiction is a great way to work your mind and learn new things. Gaining knowledge should always be a goal for you because life is about continually learning. Do not underestimate the value of a good book. Within the pages of books lie the answers to questions that you would normally ask Google!

- **Improve Your Vocabulary**

Everyone can stand to learn more words, improve their vocabulary, and become a better conversationalist. Your vocabulary and skills at expression say a lot about your knowledge, and you can enhance any conversation by being more articulate. No one says that you must learn big words to look knowledgeable, but rather, it's important to be able to employ diverse words to express your ideas. Having a diverse vocabulary will take you far in life.

- **Improve Your Memory**

If you struggle with memory, start reading and watch your memory improve. The mental stimulation that you have when you read is also increasing your ability to remember.

- **Strengthens Analytical Skills**

Being analytical is a valuable skill to have; gaining all your knowledge from television does nothing to develop your analytical skills. Learning to pore through literature or reference materials leads to adroitness and sharper mental acuity. By reading, you are improving those skills rather than tearing them down.

- **Improves Writing and Communication Skills**

Your written and communication skills are used every day of your life. Writing is valuable in most professions because it seems everybody needs to write a report, fill out applications, or perform various written tasks. Communication skills are vital in your relationships, your work, and everyday life. Being able to communicate effectively both in written and verbal form is to serve you well in your path to success.

Practical Exercises to Eliminate Distractions

Perhaps you're wondering how you can improve your focus by eliminating distractions; you may need some exercises or techniques! Eliminating distractions is going to help you concentrate on what's in front of you.

- **Turn Off Your Devices**

Your phone, tablet, and television are distractions. If you are not using any of the above for your work, turn them off and put them away. In this day and age, technology is vital to what individuals are doing. Consider other ways that you're able to complete your work if you find that you are continually distracted by the technology that you are required to use. There are apps to block sites such as social media, email; lose those distractions! Earlier, we mentioned that you should have a time limit on when and how long you can check your email and answer phone calls. This is also applicable to checking social media sites. The Internet can guzzle your time and steal your focus. By turning off your devices, you are giving yourself the chance to concentrate on the task before you fully.

- **Take Frequent Breaks**

Breaks are necessary as you go throughout your day. When you give yourself a break, you'll see your focus your concentration is improving because long runs of work without a break will "thin" your focus. Schedule breaks where you can think of something else entirely, you can leave your workspace, and give your brain a "breather." If you get caught up in your work, losing track of time, set a timer and alarm to remind it's time for a break. Remember: a five-minute break will rest your mind

- **Be Mindful of Your Physical Health**

Your physical health can affect your focus and concentration, as well. Take care of your body through proper nutrition, exercise, and minimal stress. Your body needs to be taken care of, or else everything that you work for will mean nothing. Never underestimate how valuable it is to maintain your physical well-being.

- **Remove Notifications**

Turn off notifications on your phone and all other devices. Every time you hear that ding, you are going to be tempted to check –

breaking your current train of thought. If you can't turn off your device, at least turn off the notifications.

• **Complete Your Dreaded Tasks First**

We all have tasks we dread and as hard as this is to hear: you need to tackle that dreaded task at the beginning of your day. Don't schedule it for later, because you'll spend your day with the task niggling at the back of your mind! By completing the task right away in the morning, you free your mind up in your focus to joyfully look towards everything else that you need to accomplish.

• **Eliminate Negative People from Your Life**

Negativity is another aspect of life that is going to attack your focus, your time, and your energy. Allowing negative people to dwell in your life will drain your ability to focus, and you will be constantly dragged down by the negative energy. Do not feel guilty for releasing negative relationships; your well-being needs to be a priority. Negativity has both mental and physical repercussions, and it doesn't matter if these toxic relationships are with family, friends, or co-workers – surrounding yourself with people who refuse to be positive is going to harm you. Set your sights on your goals and release any negativity in your life.

Practicing your focus and concentration is important to your success but remember the steps above and make them part of your daily routine. Invest your time in yourself and watch your focus and concentration skyrocket!

Chapter 7

Self-Esteem

Your self-esteem is a vital part of who you are, revealing how you feel about yourself and the confidence that you possess. Low self-esteem has many causes, and the goal should be to raise your self-esteem to a healthy level.

What Causes Low Self-Esteem?

Several reasons can be cited for low self-esteem. These reasons can be specific to children, adolescents, or adults. Let's look at the reasons for low self-esteem and else.

- **An Unhappy Childhood**

Adults who (as children) had caregivers who were either not involved, too involved, or too critical can experience low self-esteem later in life. Growing up being bullied or mistreated makes an individual feel unworthy. An unhappy childhood can cause you to feel like you are incapable of accomplishing your goals.

- **Mental Illness**

Certain mental illnesses, such as bipolar, depression, or anxiety, can cause you to have low self-esteem. Often these conditions are caused by a chemical imbalance in your brain or your situational condition.

It's important to seek help if you feel that you have any issues with your mental health. It's also important to understand that mental illness is not something to be ashamed of, and often has little or nothing to do with anything that you've done wrong. If your self-esteem is suffering because of mental illness, know that you are not alone, and that assistance may be a phone call away.

- **Financial Troubles**

Having issues with your financial situation can be a major blow to your self-esteem. When your finances are in trouble, the situation can lead you to blame yourself. Often financial trouble has nothing to do with anything that you've done wrong, but as something to do with external factors. When external factors are responsible, blaming yourself serves no purpose. Your self-esteem can suffer when you allow your inner critic to get the best of you and blame you for your financial situation. Before you take the blame on yourself, take time to sort through your finances, and see where the issue arose.

- **Ongoing Medical Problems**

Your physical health can cause you to have low self-esteem. If you suffer from medical issues, often you are not able to do the things that you want to do, which in turn can cause you to feel poorly about yourself. Taking care of your physical health should be a priority, but sometimes no matter what you do, you still wind up with medical issues. Remember that you cannot control everything in life.

- **Poor Treatment by Partner or Others**

Abusive situations (verbal, emotional, or physical) clearly leads to poor self-esteem. It is important to get out of the situation as soon as possible and stop enabling the abusers. In an abusive situation, the abuser is the person who has problems, not the person being abused.

- **Being Bullied**

If you are a victim of bullying, your self-esteem will be affected. Bullying causes the individual to feel unworthy and inadequate. If you are the victim of bullying, either now or in the past, it's important to talk to someone about the way you are feeling. It's important to remember that you did nothing to cause the bullying, but the important idea to remember is to seek help so that you can be on the path to rediscovering how great you are.

- **Previous Academic Challenges**

An individual who struggled academically in school is also at risk for low self-esteem. It's often hard to remember that people learn differently, and as a result, an individual can suffer if they do not keep up with their peers academically.

- **Trauma**

Like victims of abuse, victims of trauma often feel like they have done something to deserve the experience. If you have suffered a traumatic event, consider seeking help to determine how the drama is affecting you, and how to move beyond it.

- **Societal and Media Pressure**

Media creates unrealistic images of both women and men: perfect bodies, beautiful/handsome faces, the latest and best clothing, sparkling white teeth. It's no wonder that this nonviable, unfeasible portrayal of men and women in our society leads to unrealistic expectations of what our bodies, minds, and personalities need to be. Remember that those are paid models, airbrushed, and photoshopped into that myth called "perfection."

How to Boost Your Self-Confidence and Quit Sabotaging Your Life

It's common that when your self-esteem is low, and you feel poorly about yourself, you may try sabotaging anything good that happens to you. This is a common occurrence because when you feel poorly about yourself, you feel that you do not deserve goodness and happiness. To overcome these feelings and to quit sabotaging your life, consider the tips below.

- **Learn a New Skill and Master It**

Nothing says that you are competent and worthy more than learning a new skill. You have the ability to learn something new and conquer that skill. Once mastered, your self-esteem should improve, bringing feelings of validation back to you.

- **Keep a Record of Your Accomplishments**

In your journal, keep a list of everything that you've been successful at. It doesn't matter how small the task may be, write it down. When you suffer low self-esteem, it helps to remember each small detail of everything that you have done wonderfully. Stop seeking validation from others and reflect upon the accomplishments that you have made in your lifetime.

- **Be Creative**

Creativity sparks self-love. Find a way to create something. Write a poem, draw a picture, paint, or work with raw materials to create something beautiful. Creativity is wonderful because you have the power to create something from nothing! Unharness your inventive and artistic side!

- **Define Your Values**

By defining what you believe in and living by those values, you are showing who you are as a person. If you believe in love and peace, look for ways to express those values to others. Your self-esteem will improve because when you live what you believe, you have a greater chance of succeeding. Remember that embracing who you are and living the life that you want is a wonderful way to be your own person.

- **Challenge the Limiting Beliefs That You Have**

Limiting beliefs are ones that tell you cannot do something because of a trait that you have, or a skill you are missing. Examples of limiting beliefs might be: "I can't do that, I'm a woman." Why not? Women fly airplanes, repair computers, solve mysteries, save lives, and teach others how to do the same! Believing that you are limited to what you can accomplish is going to cause you to feel poorly about yourself. Releasing these beliefs and embracing true beliefs about yourself is going to affect your self-esteem positively.

- **Get Out of Your Comfort Zone**

Are you stuck in a rut? Are you living each day the same as the one before? Chances are you're going to feel bad about yourself if you remain in your comfort zone. Being where you are comfortable is good to a certain extent, but if you never venture out of that zone, you run the risk of being complacent. Taking risks allows you to grow and learn as a person, and as a result, you are going to feel better about yourself for each accomplishment.

- **Come to Terms with Your Past**

The past is behind you, and there's nothing you can do to change it. Understanding this is going to allow you to come to terms with past events and choices. Once you understand and come to terms with the choices that you've made, you are going to feel freedom. Keeping yourself bogged down by memories of poor choices serves no purpose other than to hold you back from progress. Reflect upon the past, come to terms with it, and release it. Once you do this, you have the freedom to become who you are meant to be and to accomplish great things.

- **Stop Caring What Others Think**

Carrying the burden of trying to live up to somebody else's expectations is going to hold you back. No one should be required to live a life on someone else's terms because everyone is different. Walk away from that trap; others' opinions about you and your life are just that: Their opinions. Releasing yourself from concerns about their opinions allows you to feel freedom like you never have before.

- **Integrity**

Live your life with integrity. This means to hold yourself to a high moral standard and make sure that your life reflects that. When you practice integrity, you are showing the world that you are worthwhile, that you value yourself, and that you value others.

- **Release Negative Relationships**

Negative relationships hold you back. They also affect your self-esteem, and they can keep you from reaching your true potential. Relationships that cause you mental, physical, and emotional stress and harm should be released permanently. Do not cling to those in your life who do not value you and treat you with respect. You deserve more, and once you demand that, you're going to see your self-esteem improve.

- **Value Your Appearance**

When you put a value on your outward appearance, you show the world that you care about yourself. This does not mean being in the height of fashion, but rather, it means being properly groomed, clean, and neat. Taking care of how you look is going to make you feel better about yourself and show the world that you value who you are.

- **Embrace Failure and Grow from It**

Everyone fails at some point in life; those who say otherwise are likely lying. Failure is nothing more than an opportunity to learn and grow. Each time you feel like you failed at something, look for the learning opportunity. Embrace these opportunities and valuable life lessons. When you do that, and you reframe your negative thoughts about failure, you are going to feel better about yourself. By growing as an individual, you understand that you have the ability to move on and be greater when you were before.

- **Continue to Learn**

Just like mastering a new skill, learning continually boosts your self-esteem. Each new fact or tidbit that you learn is expanding your mind and growing you as an individual. Take pride in this! Not everyone makes it a practice to continue learning past traditional schooling. Expanding your mind is a good way to improve your self-esteem.

- **Embrace Your Fears**

Living life in a fearful state is no way to live. By embracing your fears and learning to act regardless of them, you are showing the world that you are resilient and strong. When you embrace your fears, you are going to feel better about yourself as you realize that nothing can hold you back.

- **Define Success for You**

Success looks different for each individual. Take the time to clearly define what success is going to look like for you. From there, reach for that success by setting goals that will help you along the journey, finding the determination to achieve each one of them. As you check the goals off your list, feel your self-esteem improve because you know that nothing is holding you back.

Understanding Who You Are

Self-awareness is vital to your success and will affect your mindset. It is also vital to understand who you are so that you can improve your self-esteem and maintain how you feel about yourself.

- **Embrace Your Feelings**

Feelings, whether they are positive or negative, affect who we are. Embrace every feeling and emotion that you have. We are taught from an early age that we need to hide or negative emotions, but this was a lie. Negative emotions have a place for expression in our lives, but we need to make sure that we are doing this appropriately. Use your positive and your negative emotions to your advantage and harness the energy that they produce. These emotions can drive you to be a better person and achieve your goals.

- **Seek Out Feedback**

Feedback is a great way for us to grow as individuals. Ask your boss, your coworkers, or your partner how you can improve. Remember, though: this is feedback, and this feedback is based on opinions. You need to compare the opinions of others to the facts that you know about yourself before making any changes.

- **Understand Your Strengths and Weaknesses**

We talked about understanding what your weaknesses are so that you can improve, but it's just important for you to understand what your strengths are as well. Knowing who you are, what you're good at, and where you need improvement is important to your self-esteem. Understand what you are good at so that you can take pride in those activities and tasks, but don't forget about areas needing improvement! Addressing each of those areas is going to boost your self-esteem.

- **Be Mindful**

Practicing mindfulness requires that you remain in the moment. Do not allow your mind to wander to past decisions or to worry about the future. Be mindful of who you are, where you are at in life, and where you are going. Everything else does not require your attention at the moment. When you focus on who you are right now, your self-esteem is going to improve because you can see that you are working towards your success.

- **Remain Open-Minded**

It's important to keep an open mind about new ideas, people, and places. Being open-minded is going to ensure that you are looking at different perspectives which - in turn – helps you avoid becoming judgmental. When you are open-minded, this benefits your self-esteem because you are making better choices.

Visualization

Visualization is an effective technique that allows you to see the results and experience them before they happen. There are several tips and techniques that you can use to practice visualization. Below you will find some effective strategies for making visualization part of your life.

- **Use Affirmations and Expect Results**

Affirmations are highly effective statements that allow you to trigger positive feelings within your mind., activating the Law of Attraction. These positive statements proclaim what you expect every day: I will succeed. I am worthwhile. I will reach my goals.

- **Index Cards**

Use index cards to record each goal you have, keeping them near your bed and going through them one at a time. With each visualization, spend 15 seconds imagining the result of these goals. Make sure that you are doing this regularly until your goals are achieved.

- **Create Goal Pictures**

Goal pictures are a photo or up drawing showing yourself reaping the benefits of reaching your goals. Study these, imagine that you are there, your goal achieved! You can draw yourself in a drawing, or you can use Photoshop to put yourself into the photo. Some examples would be taking a picture of yourself at a car dealership behind the wheel of your dream car and photoshopping yourself into an office space that the picture exactly what you want. This is an effective way to see exactly what you want your life to look like.

- **For Each Picture Attached in Affirmation**

Each photo or picture that you have depicting yourself achieving your goals should have an affirmation attached to it. This is effective because when you repeat that affirmation, it will not matter if you have the pictures in front of you are not because the affirmation is going to bring that goal to mind. The benefits of visualizing yourself completing your goals are numerous.

- **Activating Creativity**

When you use visualization, you are allowing yourself to take a creative approach to complete your goals. Visualization requires you to use your imagination.

- **Programs Your Brain to Recognize What You Need to Achieve Your Dreams**

Visualization is an exercise that trains your brain to recognize what you need (or need to do) to achieve your dreams. Think of this as an exercise where you are building the willpower and the stamina needed to complete a goal. As you visualize, you are looking at each step that needs to be taken so that you can accomplish this in real life.

- **Activates the Law of Attraction**

Remember that the Law of Attraction means that you are manifesting whatever it is you desire from life. You can manifest money, thoughts, actions, and more. The universe will give you what you desire if you practice a positive mindset.

- **Builds Internal Motivation**

Being internally motivated is important. When you rely on factors outside of yourself for motivation, you're going to be disappointed. Recognition, awards, and bonuses are nice, but learn to rely on your internal motivation to serve you well throughout your lifetime as you pursue your goals. The satisfaction that you get from achieving your goals should be enough.

Your self-esteem is important to who you are and how you achieve your goals. You need to make sure that you are taking care of yourself and doing everything you can to boost your self-esteem. View yourself as worthy, important, and deserving of the best life has to offer!

Chapter 8

Mental Toughness

Being mentally tough means that you can withstand constructive criticism, disappointment, and failure. Mental toughness keeps you going when the going gets rough; you can continue pursuing your goals despite the setbacks you experience.

Characteristics of Mentally Tough Individuals

Perhaps you will surprise yourself and find that you already have the characteristics of somebody who is mentally tough. On the other hand, you could learn new ways that are going to benefit you throughout your lifetime.

- **Confidence**

When you believe in yourself, you have one of the basic characteristics of mental toughness. You understand that you will succeed because of who you are, the abilities (natural or obtained) that you have, and because you have self-confidence. Confidence is vital to mental toughness because you need to believe that you *can* succeed in order *to* succeed.

- **Confident in Challenges**

A person with mental toughness understands that to grow continually, one needs to be willing to learn from the challenges that are set before him. He/she understandings that focusing on achieving positive outcomes leads to success. By understanding that challenges are necessary to grow, your idea of "success" may change. While "success" looks different to everybody, a mentally tough individual realizes that part of success involves learning from the obstacles being faced.

- **Control**

Mentally tough individuals understand that the power to shape their destiny lies within them; they control their lives and their destiny - life does not control them. They have full confidence in the control they possess in terms of their life's success, and they bask in this knowledge.

- **Commitment**

The commitment of an individual with mental toughness is insurmountable. They understand that setting goals is an important step, and that facing adversity head-on makes then the victor. There is no reason to shy away from challenges or adversity when you are committed to doing what you need to do to achieve your goals.

Practicing Mental Toughness

Perhaps at this point time, you are wondering how to practice and improve mental toughness. Read the tips below and set yourself up for success!

- **Set Goals**

You've heard this in previous chapters; make a commitment by setting goals. This messages the universe that you are willing to do what it takes to be successful. You know what you want out of life, and you are going to create that no matter how hard the path may be.

- **Set Yourself Up for Success**

How do you go about setting yourself up for success? It's not complicated! To be successful, you need to learn, you need to seek feedback for improvement, you need to understand how to reshape your thought processes, and you need to be willing to make changes as necessary. By now, I'm sure you have already begun the process of setting yourself up for success. If you haven't, now is the perfect time to begin.

- **Embrace Discomfort for the Greater Good**

Growing hurts. It doesn't matter if it's something that you want, growing as an individual is going to be uncomfortable. You must face realities about yourself that you may not be fully prepared to consider. Even if this is the case, you understand that improvement begins with the discomfort of knowing you need to grow. Embrace this discomfort and know that it is going to lead to something better.

- **Reframe Your Negative Thought Processes**

As we discussed, negativity serves no purpose in your life other than to hold you back. Learn to reframe negative thought processes by stopping negative thoughts in their tracks. When you experience a negative thought, make a conscious effort to switch that negative thought into a positive one. The more you practice this, the easier it gets!

- **Balance Out Your Emotions with Logic**

Logic needs to win out above your emotions. Emotions are volatile and can often lead you down the wrong path. Each time you feel yourself getting highly emotional, make a conscious effort to slow down and let logic kick in. As you practice this, it becomes second nature to reign in your emotions, living life with a logical approach, not fleeting emotions.

- **Fulfill Your Purpose**

You need to figure out what you are meant to do. Are you meant to be a writer? Perhaps you are meant to lead a successful business? You need to take the time to determine your purpose(s) in life so that you can get busy *being* the person you are meant to be. Life will not have meaning until you live to your true potential.

- **Explanations, Not Excuses**

Mentally tough individuals do not deal with excuses. They may have explanations for why they failed or why they succeeded, but these are not to be confused with excuses. Excuses place blame and explanations accept responsibility. Individuals who display mental toughness understand that they need to accept responsibility for their actions and their choices, whether it leads to success or failure.

- **Try One Hard Task Daily**

You cannot be a wimp if you hope to succeed. You need to try hard tasks, or else you are not challenging yourself. Mentally tough individuals understand that a challenge is a way for them to grow. Each day, strive to be successful at one task that you find hard for you, sticking with it for at least ten minutes. In these ten minutes, give yourself a pep talk, boosting your motivation and building momentum to finish. Mentally tough individuals understand that finishing is important, and success is not necessarily important.

- **Take Satisfaction in Proving Yourself Wrong**

When you doubt yourself, enjoy the moment when you are proven wrong. It's no fun to be proven wrong by somebody else but take great satisfaction when you prove yourself wrong! Being wrong means that you are capable of more than you think you are. Mentally strong individuals embrace their strengths and their weaknesses because they know that both are going to play to their advantage and are important to their success.

Developing Positive Habits

To develop mental toughness, you need first to begin developing positive habits. Mentally tough individuals understand that positive habits are going to take them far in life. They work hard to develop these habits and incorporate them into their daily routine.

- **Act as If You Are in Control**

Even when you are not in control, you must act as if you are! When life feels like it is spiraling out of control, it is important to maintain the façade that you are in control and life is not. As the phrase goes: "Fake it 'til you make it!" This is important when you are dealing with control. Believe that you have control of your life and your situation even when you feel completely useless. The control will come in time but pretending that you have it is going to give you the confidence to proceed until you are once again in control.

- **Discard What You Have No Control Over**

There is no point in holding onto something that is out of your control; you are only hurting yourself. Time and energy are going to be wasted on a situation, task, or projects that you have no control over. Make sure that you identify early on if something is within your control or not, and you will see your outcomes change from negative to positive.

- **The Past can Provide Valuable Training**

Your past is nothing but a series of lessons that you learn from life. Do not dwell on the past but rather take the life lessons and treat them as a training exercise. Learning to be objective about your past helps you see the valuable training that you had within you all along. Remember that each failure or disappointment is nothing more than a learning exercise and does not reflect on you as a person.

- **Celebrate Others Success**

Mentally tough individuals understand the importance of celebrating the success of other people. By celebrating the success of other individuals, you understand that their success plays no part in yours. Celebrate each accomplishment that people in your life achieve because when you achieve your success, those same individuals are going to be there cheering you on. Remember that others succeeding does not mean you are going to fail.

- **Stop Complaining, Whining, and Criticizing**

Complaining means that you're not willing to do the work to achieve the outcome that you want. Whining shows that you are not accepting responsibility for your part. Criticizing only serves the purpose of making you appear less grateful and bitter about other people's success. Complaining, whining, and criticizing is only going to bring you down, turning your mindset negative. Remember the importance of a positive mindset as you are trying to fulfill your goals.

- **Impress Only Yourself**

You do not need to impress other individuals in life. The only person that you should set out to impress is yourself because your opinion matters - other people's opinions don't. When you set out to impress only yourself, you are going to find that you are more satisfied in life and that your success is that much sweeter. Mentally strong individuals understand that the opinions of others do not matter, taking those opinions with a grain of salt, comparing them to the facts they know about themselves and their lives. If they find themselves coming up short, they know that all they can do is strive to improve.

- **Count Your Blessings**

Being grateful is an important part of achieving your dreams. Practicing a grateful attitude shows others the importance of knowing exactly where you are in life. The blessings that you have been given help in driving you towards success; grateful people understand the importance of hard work and discipline.

- **Develop Emotional Intelligence**

Emotional intelligence involves using your own emotions to your advantage, understanding the emotions of others and basing your actions on that understanding. Emotional intelligence is important as a skill because when you can relate better to the emotions that other people are feeling, your interpersonal relationships are going to improve. A large part of emotional intelligence is empathy. Empathy requires that you look at different perspectives and try to view life from another person's point of view.

- **Say No**

Learning to say no is another valuable tool in your arsenal. Saying "no" is not rude, and you are not showing less care for other people. In reality, you are showing other people that you value your time and your energy. By saying no, you are staying true to your values, and you are living life according to those values. Be sure to give a reason when you say "no" so that others' understand you have a valid reason. Refuse to do activities or take on tasks that do not align with your goals or your values.

- **Fear is the Only Reason to Regret**

The only reason that you should regret a past decision is if it was driven by fear. Remember that you need to overcome your fears to succeed.

- **Embrace Failure and Let Go of Mistakes**

Failure is an opportunity to learn, and when you realize that you are going to see that your mindset changes. Mentally strong individuals understand the importance of embracing their failure in releasing past mistakes. Mistakes provide a pathway to learning. Think of when you are learning to walk or ride a bike. When you fell, did you give up, or did you continue to try? If you gave up chances are you would not be reading this book. I'm going to go out on a limb and say that you continued to try. You probably did not realize that when you were learning to ride a bike, each time you fell you were making mental assessments of what went wrong *that* time! Life is similar; when you learn from your mistakes, you will find that it is easier to let them go.

- **Forgive**

To be successful and healthy as an individual, you need to practice forgiveness. Forgiveness is important to extend to others who may have wronged you or made poor choices that affected you. This is also important for you to practice with yourself. Make sure that when you slip up or you make a mistake that you are forgiving yourself and moving on.

- **Remain Positive**

Positivity can be hard to maintain unless you are mentally strong. Mental toughness allows you to keep a positive attitude even when you feel like the world is falling around you. Try to keep an optimistic view of life, your goals, and your relationships. This is going to allow you to be more successful and achieve your dreams.

Advantages to Mental Strength

Being mentally tough has its advantages, and below you'll find a few (in case you need to be convinced to develop this skill!)

- **Develops Leadership Skills**

Later in the book, we are going to talk about leadership and how being mentally tough is related. Leadership skills required that you can take criticism, feedback, and tough situations without crumbling. Mental toughness allows you to remain a positive leader despite the circumstances around you.

- **Conquers Doubt**

Doubting yourself is not going to serve any purpose when setting out to achieve goals and be successful in life. With a positive mindset and mental toughness, you can quiet the doubt that you may be feeling and instead embrace the positive success that is coming your way.

- **Develop and Maintain Motivation**

Mental toughness gives you the ability to switch from being externally motivated to being internally motivated. Internal motivation is something you drive; external motivation is being driven by someone else. When you rely on external factors to drive you to be successful, you are going to be disappointed. Learning mental toughness is going to allow you to develop an internal motivation which will help you on your journey to conquering your goals.

- **Unhelpful Advice**

Unhelpful feedback serves no purpose other than squashing your spirit. Mental toughness allows you to filter out the unhelpful advice and keep only the helpful recommendations that come your way.

- **Helps You Learn from Your Mistakes**

Being mentally tough is going to allow you to take the lessons from your mistakes and apply them to your life. When you get a handle on this, remember learning from your mistakes allows you to release them. There's no reason to dwell on mistakes other than to learn the lesson and let them go.

- **Gives You the Courage to Face Your Fears**

Mentally tough individuals understand that facing their fears is the only way that they can proceed forward. Make sure that you understand how important it is to treat fear as a motivator and not as a hindrance. To be successful, you need to take the energy from your fear and apply it to the situation. When you can learn to do that, you will have achieved a certain level of mental toughness that is going to see you being successful throughout your life.

Being mentally tough is vital to your life because, without it, you are going to struggle to accomplish your goals. Adopting the right mindset and learning how to remain mentally strong will help you in your relationships, in life, and in your career.

Chapter 9

Social Intelligence

Your social skills are something that you need to continually develop throughout your lifetime. Without effective social skills, you are going to struggle in your relationships, in your career, and in life in general. Understanding how to become socially intelligent is an important part of growing.

Communication: The Backbone of Relationships

Some people enjoy communicating, and others find it tiresome. No matter which person you are, it is important that you develop your communication skills so that you can be an effective person in life.

- **Make It a Priority**

Your communicating style needs your scrutiny! Once you have determined how you communicate best, make it a priority to hone the skills and leave the flaws behind. Increase your vocabulary, practice your written message, and work on your speaking skills. By making communication a priority, you are going to learn how to best engage other individuals.

- **Simplify Your Message and Stay on Track**

Verbally rattling on and on about your message or becoming sidetracked and telling random stories is not effective communication. When somebody's listening to you, it is courteous to be sure you clear, concise, and stay on point. Remember that unless the message is delivered effectively, it will lose its meaning.

- **Engage Your Listeners**

Asking questions and allowing the people who are listening to you to respond is a good way to keep them engaged in what you're saying. Remember how important it is to keep people engaged in your message; if you forget to keep them interested, your message is going to get lost. When you set out to communicate with someone, it's important to make sure that you are respectful to their needs as well.

- **Respond to Them**

Speaking of being respectful to your audience's needs, it's important that you respond to questions, comments, and body language. Notice if they seem uncomfortable or uninterested, changing directions and re-engaging them as necessary. When you are responsive to your audience, you'll find they are more responsive to you as well.

- **Make Sure You Are Understood**

Avoid being vague, or you risk the chance that you will be misunderstood. If your topic happens to be a delicate one, it is more important than ever that you ensure that your audience understands what you're trying to convey. Avoid off-color jokes, and keep the message audience-appropriate.

- **Develop Listening Skills**

As you are learning to communicate with others, it's important that you also learn how to listen. Active listening involves making sure that your mind does not wander, ensuring that you are receiving the appropriate message, and maintaining eye contact with the speaker.

Active listening is going to serve you well throughout your lifetime, so consider honing this skill as soon as possible.

- **Use Appropriate Body Language**

Body language is important. When you are communicating with others, it's important to be mindful of not only the audience's body language but your body language as well. Standing with your arms crossed, for example, indicates that you are either angry, bored, or disinterested. Rolling your eyes is a sign of disrespect and gives the indication that you do not agree, or you want to disengage from the conversation. Make sure your body language matches the tone of your voice, being mindful of your facial expressions as well. Smiling during a sad story is inappropriate. Ber mindful to display proper emotions and be willing to work on your body language during communication.

- **Maintain Eye Contact**

Making or maintaining eye contact can be affected by the individual's background. Some cultures find it rude to maintain eye contact with the speaker. In American culture, it is considered rude not to maintain eye contact when somebody is speaking. Eye contact seen as a way to show that you are engaged in your listening. Based on your cultural preferences, try to maintain eye contact with the speaker to show that you are listening, and you are engaged in what they are saying.

What Was Your Name? Tips to Remember Names

Do you have a hard time remembering names? I do! If you struggle with remembering names, especially right after they were given to you, this section is for you. Below you will find some tips to help you remember and improve your social intelligence.

- **Make the Commitment to Remember Names**

You must make a commitment to strengthening your name-recalling skills, going the extra mile, using all the resources available to you.

This commitment to remember names shows that you value relationships - even the new ones that you have just made.

- **Concentrate and Focus on The Person You Are Speaking To**

This is especially important when you are meeting new individuals. When you are in a conversation with someone else, it's important that you maintain focus and you concentrate on what the person is saying. This becomes vital when engaging with someone that you do not know. Make an effort to remain mindful during a conversation. This is going to help you link the name and the conversation that you had with the individual.

- **Repeat the Person's Name**

This is a tip that it seems everybody has heard. When you say hello, it is important to repeat the person's name: "Hello, John. Nice to meet you!" This habit helps solidify the name in your mind.

- **Make an Association Between the Name and The Person**

Associating somebody's name with a trait that they have is another good way to remember. Try to find a link between the name and the person's face, for example: "Cass with the glasses." How you associate the face with the name is up to you but find a trick that's going to help you remember his or her name.

- **Don't Have Another Conversation in Your Head**

This goes along with focusing and concentrating on the person that is speaking. When you focus on what the other person is saying, you cannot have another conversation in your head. Additionally, this keeps you from rehearsing your response while the other person is still speaking. Be courteous and remain mindful and at the moment when another person is speaking. This is going to ensure that you are able to remember their name because you are more likely to remember the conversation.

- **Repeat the Name When You Say Goodbye**

We already discussed repeating the name right after you meet the individual. It's also important to repeat the name as you tell them goodbye – just another step towards cementing their name in your ind. It's also helpful to repeat the person's name during the conversation but try not to make it awkward. It's also perfectly acceptable to repeat the name a few times and make a joke about how you are horrible with names. This helps break the ice, and it also helps the other person understand that you value them because you are trying to remember their name.

- **Review New Names at The End of The Day**

If you are in the business of meeting new people on a continual basis, a good practice to adopt is reviewing new names at the end of the day. Picture the name and the person and keep that association strong. The likelihood that you will remember them later one grows each time you are able to link their name to their face.

Improve Your Presentation Skills

To be an effective presenter, you need to practice. Plan out your presentation and make a point to practice more than twice. Practice in front of the mirror, practice in front of other people, record yourself practicing, and then view the results. As you look at yourself during the presentation, make notes, pay attention to your body language, and work on your expressions. The practice is vital to making your presentation flawless and effective.

- **Transform Nervous Energy into Enthusiasm**

Do you struggle with public speaking? If so, you understand what nervous energy is. Ignore the nervous part of that energy and transform it into enthusiasm. It's important that you appear enthusiastic even if you have butterflies floating around inside you.

The most effective way to do that is to pretend that you are as enthusiastic as you would like your audience to view you.

- **Watch Other Presenters**

If you're presenting at a conference, watch other presentations, gauging the reaction of the audience and tweaking your own presentation based on those observations. If you don't have the opportunity to view other speakers in person, watch Ted talks or how-to videos on YouTube. Note and incorporate into your own presentation the positive habits of speakers, also taking note of any negative tendencies you can avoid in your own presentation.

- **Arrive Early**

Make an appointment arrived early to assess the environment around you, greeting people as they enter, making sure to engage a few of them. Arriving early allows you to look at your surroundings and calmly begin your presentation without feeling rushed.

- **Smile**

Smiling is the most important thing that you can do when you're presenting. By smiling, you're giving yourself a chance to feel as confident as you are trying to portray. A smile causes you to relax and connects you with your audience.

- **Use Positive Visualization**

We have discussed how important visualization is, and when you use positive visualization to gauge and determine how your presentation is going to go, you've just upped your success rate. It's important to visualize what could go wrong and try to envision how you would react to that. As you're going through your speech, visualizing how the audience is going to respond, it's important that you are also adding in some setbacks or obstacles that could potentially interrupt your presentation. Envision how you're going to react, and this is going to help you already have a pattern in your mind about what could go wrong and what could go right. Knowing how you would react in different situations is a good way to prepare yourself and to calm yourself beforehand.

- **Remember to Breathe Deeply**

Breathing deeply is an effective way to calm yourself down. Before you start your presentation, make sure that you are taking a few deep breaths so that you give yourself a chance to get acclimated to your surroundings. If during your speech you begin to feel nervous or you get jittery, take a moment to pause. An effective and well-timed pause gives the appearance of confidence when, in reality, you are just giving yourself a chance to catch up.

- **Don't Cover Too Much Material**

When covering how to improve your social skills, I mentioned the importance of simplifying your message and staying on track. This applies to presentations as well. Be specific in what you're talking about, and do not cover too much material or you may bore your audience. Your objective in giving a presentation is to deliver information in an engaging manner so that the people can learn as much as they can without falling asleep!

- **Work on Pausing**

Pauses can be an effective part of presentations. By inserting pauses appropriately, you not only provide an opportunity to gather your thoughts, you are giving the audience a chance to digest your message. When practicing your presentation, consider optimal places you can incorporate effective pauses.

- **Encourage Audience Interaction**

As you begin your speech, encourage interaction with your audience. This helps them understand your message and gives you a chance to see if you need to change direction in delivery. Encourage questions and comments as a way to keep your audience from zoning out.

- **Be Entertaining**

No one likes to sit through a presentation with a person who speaks in a monotone, delivering dull fact after dull fact. Toss in some personal stories, jokes, or other lighthearted material that allows your audience to take a mental break while you are speaking.

- **Admit That You Don't Know Everything**

No one has all the answers, so admit that in the beginning of your presentation. Your humility assures the audience that while you know quite a bit on the topic, you do not expect them to believe you know everything.

- **Use A Powerful Stance**

This tip is handy *before you go up on stage.* Stand in the Superman pose, putting your hands on your hips, sticking your chest out, and looking upwards with confidence. Practice the stance for 30 seconds before you go in front of your audience, and you will find that you feel more confident as you go forward.

- **Drink Water**

Hydration is important, especially when giving a presentation. Do not be afraid to take a glass or water bottle with you on stage; it may give you a moment to pause, gather your thoughts, and reassess your approach, if necessary. If you are speaking for a long time, it's very important to remain hydrated so that you don't feel faint or sick throughout your presentation. That said, don't overdo it or you may find yourself needing to take an unexpected bathroom break!

- **Embrace the Fear**

Do you have a fear of public speaking? Many people do, and the problem with that is that you doubt your own competence. The chances are that you would not have been asked to speak if other people did not view you as an expert in your field. Transform that fear into confidence by accepting the fact that others see you as competent in your field. Recite that to yourself before you go on stage and use affirmations to ensure success.

The Art of Constructive Feedback

If you are in a position of leadership, constructive feedback is vital to that role. Even if you're not in the position of leadership, understanding constructive feedback is going to serve you in your relationships.

- **Focus on The Problem and Be Specific**

If you are giving constructive feedback, chances are you are giving this feedback in relation to a problem or an or an issue that needs to be addressed. Make sure that you focus on the problem, staying specific in terms of why this is a problem; this is no time to be vague.

- **Discuss the Situation – not the Individual**

Effective feedback concentrates on the situation or the problem that needs to be addressed. Do not make this about the person you are speaking to, running the risk of ruining the feedback you intent to provide. Discussing the situation allows the person to see what was done wrong, instead of centering on how they were wrong. Focus on the problem, not the person.

- **Give Praise When Needed**

It is vital that you praise the individual when the situation calls for it. Even if you are in the position of having to use feedback to correct the situation, find a way to give praise, boosting their confidence, solidifying your relationship, and ensuring that the feedback is received properly.

- **Be Direct, but Keep an Informal Attitude**

Formality and stiffness can hinder feedback reception. Address the situation directly but do so in an informal way. An example: rather than meeting in a formal office or conference room, sit across from the individual without any obstruction between you. This allows you to appear more informal and gives the illusion that you and the individual are merely having a conversation. Make sure that when you are delivering feedback that you are sitting and relaxed. Be mindful of your body language and ensure that you are not delivering the wrong message. Your words and your body language need to match up.

- **Be Sincere**

People can pick up on insincerity. No one enjoys being spoken to and treated in a condescending manner. When you are insincere, you come across as condescending, and this can damage your relationship with the other individual. Make sure that what you say is what you mean, and make sure that your tone matches your words.

- **Listen**

Feedback is only constructive if you're listening to what the other individual is saying. Giving the other person the opportunity to speak and share their opinion reduces the chance of them feeling attacked.

- **Be Timely**

Do not wait too long to deliver constructive feedback. If the feedback is related to a specific incident, it's important that you address the incident quickly and not wait too long.

- **Focus on How to Change and Point Out Opportunities**

When giving constructive feedback, it's important that you focus on the change that needs to be made and the opportunities that the individual has to make these changes. When you focus on change in opportunity, your feedback is going to come across as positive and will be received better. By focusing on change and opportunities, you are ensuring that the individual is going to take your comments to heart, and actually look forward to the changes that they can make.

- **Prepare the Person for The Feedback**

When delivering feedback, it doesn't hurt to prepare the person. Using a phrase such as "you may not like what I have to say" or "This may be hard to hear, but it's necessary" can help prepare the individual for what may be difficult feedback. No matter how much you want them to receive the feedback positively, there is always a chance that the person will not see any positivity in your conversation. The person may believe that you are attacking them and close down emotionally. Remember to give some thought to how you might prepare the other person for this difficult conversation.

- **Make the Conversation Private**

Nobody likes to be corrected in public! Make sure that you are in an informal setting, but also that there is privacy. This allows the other person to focus on what you are saying and not who is listening. This is a respectful approach.

- **Begin by Pointing Out the Good**

Do not start out with negative feedback, but rather start out with the positive qualities of the individual. This opens the lines of communication which are going to be important throughout the conversation.

- **Maintain Communication**

After you've delivered your feedback, make sure that you keep the lines of communication open. Offer opportunities to state opinions – even if those opinions are in direct disagreement with your position. Giving the other person the option to speak ensures that even after the feedback is given, the lines of communication are going to remain open.

- **Discuss Action**

Let the individual know that there is an action that they can take, providing opportunities that are available to them. Empowering the other individual to take action on their own behalf is a good form of leadership. Leaders understand that empowerment is going to serve them better than tearing an individual down. Lay out steps to correct the situation and make them action oriented.

- **Remain Objective and Respectful**

Do not allow your personal feelings to enter into the conversation. Keep your perspective objective, respecting the person as an individual and understanding that their emotions and their needs play a part in that conversation. You are showing your skills as an effective leader when giving respect along with constructive feedback.

- **Use Your Emotional Intelligence**

This is vital because when you understand what the other person is feeling, you are able to act accordingly. Navigating their feelings as you provide feedback shows emotional intelligence! Before you begin the conversation, make sure that you have considered the other person's perspective.

Your social skills are going to determine the success of your relationships, the work that you do, and the opportunities that present themselves throughout your lifetime. Keep in mind that your social skills require a lifetime of commitment to practicing and improving them.

Chapter 10

Leadership Skills

Are you currently a leader in your profession? Perhaps you are someone who desires to be a leader? If so, this chapter is for you! We will discuss the different types of leadership, learn what your superpower is, and effective leadership skills you'll need to become successful. Here are some valuable tips on how to bravely embrace leadership.

Learning Your Superpower

Your superpower is simply something that you do well and with passion. Do you already know your superpower? Perhaps you are on a quest to find your superpower: read on. We are going to learn how to find the superpower within us and use that superpower to better our circumstances.

- **List What You Do Well**

The first step in discovering your superpower is understanding what it is that you do well. List everything that you do well, even if it is simply cleaning the toilet. Each task that you can perform to near perfection should be on this list. You should feel empowered by this list, your self-esteem should be boosted, and there should be nothing on this list that makes you feel bad about yourself.

- **What Comes Naturally?**

From that superpower list, which activities and tasks come naturally to you? Pick out each ability listed that you can do with your eyes closed. It's something that you just automatically know how to do without thinking. Create a separate list from the first one, considering each ability that you naturally possess. We will keep creating lists and eventually narrow them down until we discover your superpower!

- **What Are You Passionate About?**

On that second list, cross out everything that you are not passionate about. Anything on that list that doesn't set a fire burning in your soul – cross it off! Consider each option thoroughly because this is an important activity.

- **Which of These Items Makes Time Disappear?**

As you are thinking about your list, write down anything that you are able to do that makes time simply disappeared. What is something that you do where you can lose track of time entirely? This is an activity that you cannot start if you have another responsibility later. If you engage in this activity and have an appointment you must go to, you understand that you must set an alarm to break the focus and concentration required by this activity! For example, you might be painting, writing, giving a friend advice; whatever the activity, it comes naturally to you and you are deeply passionate about it.

- **What Makes You Different?**

This is an interesting way to understanding your superpower because now we need to look at what makes you slightly different - or perhaps a lot different - from your peers. Each of us has an ability that makes us just a little bit different than everybody else. There is a likelihood that more than one ability is going to come to mind. Ensure that you are paying attention and that you are taking your time to think these lists through. This is not something that you are going to accomplish in a day, but rather this is something that may take some time; that's fine. It's important to look at the different abilities, skills, and strengths that you have that are going to set you apart from the other people.

- **Consider Why Others Would Seek Advice from You**

Perhaps you are a skilled writer, and your friends and family often seek your advice when they must prepare a report, write a letter, or create a resume. Perhaps you have exceptional people skills, allowing you to easily read others' emotions, see their perspective, or anticipate how they are going to react to different situations. Think about time people asked for your advice: what were you giving advice on? List those things and proceed to the next step.

- **When You Were a Child, What Did You Love to Do?**

This one is a fun and exciting step. Think back to when you were a child all the way up through your teen years, considering what you enjoyed doing the most. It's a very interesting concept because what you enjoy doing as a child is going to translate into what you are going to do as an adult. Each activity that you had as a child is preparing you for adulthood. Consider if you enjoyed imaginative play. How is this going to translate into an adult skill? Perhaps this makes you a writer, this could make you an actress or an actor, or this could make you an effective presenter. Notice how one's skill can give you many different superpowers. Make a list of everything that you enjoyed doing as a child – leave nothing out!

- **If Money Was No Object…**

Take your time to consider what you would do with your life if you didn't have to worry about money? Would you begin a career speaking on topics that you are passionate about? Would you teach children or adults? Consider each activity or task that you would do if you didn't need a paycheck.

- **Look at The Answer That Is on Each List**

Some items are going to pop up on the different lists you have created. You may find yourself crossing off some items as they become less applicable. Consider how these skills are interrelated. Look at how you are able to use them in daily life. How do these translate into real-life situations?

Have you come up with your superpower from your list? This exercise is important because if you do not find the correlation between what you do well, what you enjoy doing, and what comes naturally to you, you are not going to discover your superpower. Look at the individual qualities, abilities, and skills that you have and make them translate into a real-life situation. Chances are you're going to have several options and these options are going to be crystal clear by the end of this activity. I wish you luck in finding your superpower, and I hope you find all the success in the world once you have discovered why you have this strange collection of skills and abilities.

Types of Leadership

There are six different types of leadership; determine which type of leader you are and apply that leadership type to the next few sections of the book. Once you figure out how to apply your leadership style to your life, you are going to see that success finds you.

- **Democratic Leadership**

The democratic leadership style invites participation from team members. When making decisions, the democratic leader is going to seek advice and opinions from team members and incorporate those into decision-making.

- **Autocratic Leadership**

This type of leadership style is an aggressive personality who seeks to the power to control everyone and everything involved, making decisions without consulting team members. These types of leaders often demand work and expect the results immediately. This is a very strong individual and their personality tends to be overpowering.

- **Coaching Leadership**

This is the most ideal and most effective type of leadership, allowing for empowerment rather than control. These leaders lead indirectly.

- **Strategic Leadership**

This leadership style is one that can influence the success of others and represents another type of empowering leadership.

- **Transformational Leadership**

This leader creates a thriving work environment, using effective communication and allowing team members to interject their opinions on important matters.

What's your leadership style? Is it effective? Read on to compare your leadership style to the effective leadership skills shown below.

Effective Leadership and The Skills That You Need

To lead effectively, you need to have a variety of skills in your arsenal so that you are able to make use of your team members and their abilities.

- **Have a Vision**

It's important that you know what you want, where you are going, and how you are going to get there. This is important in your personal life but it is also vital if you are leading others. Make sure that you communicate your vision with your team members, reminding them of this vision as you lead.

- **Lead by Example**

Do not expect people to follow the lead of someone who expects others to meet standards that he feels do not apply to himself. Become an example of the type of individual you want on your team. A leader is someone that empowers and inspires others to follow them. Consider how you lead: is it by example or is it "Do as I say, not as I do"?

- **Displaying Integrity**

Integrity means living and leading with a strong moral compass. If you are a leader, integrity is vital. Make sure that your life reflects the integrity that is within you. If it does not, consider making some changes. Effective leaders display integrity and they live their life as an example to others.

- **Effectively Communicate**

The chapter on communication was important your personal life but it is even more important if you are a leader. Learning how to communicate effectively is going to inspire change in your team members and it will empower them as well. Use all of the effective communication skills that you have in your toolkit and you will see success through your team members.

- **Make the Tough Calls**

Leaders can make calls that may be unpopular and that may result in criticism. As a leader, you need to be able to make these tough calls. Tough calls can include firing someone, adopting a policy that may be unpopular, or simply adopting a schedule that may leave others unhappy. You are a leader for a reason, and you need to lead by example. Your goal is to empower, not be popular.

- **Acknowledge Success**

As a leader, it is important for you to pay attention to successful results. You need to seek out the individuals that are consistently bringing in successful outcomes. This is going to endear your team members to you because they know that you appreciate the work that they are doing. As a leader, this is an important skill; your team members need to have confidence that you are seeing what is happening around you. As you acknowledge the success of those around you, you are going to see the outcomes of your team members improve.

- **Empower Others**

Empowering others is an important part of leadership. Give your team members the tools that they need to be successful. Empowering them involves setting them up for success, and then praising them when they achieve this. Think of leaders who have empowered you to be better and to move on in life.

- **Motivate and Inspire**

We have discussed the importance of internal motivation is, but when you are a leader it is your job to offer extra motivation. This can be in the form of acknowledgments, bonuses, or simply better tasks to complete. It never hurts to motivate your team members to improve and work harder. Oftentimes this happens when you offer some sort of external reward. Being inspirational is something that you need to work on because inspiring your team members is just as important as and motivating them. Give them a reason for successful outcomes and watch the environment around you change! An inspiring and motivating leader can change a work environment from poor to excellent with little effort. Strive to be that leader.

- **Persuasion and Influence**

How are you at using your influence to get results? Influence and persuasion simply mean that you can use your skills, abilities, and work effectively to make others do what you want them to do. Sometimes persuasion and influence are used in a negative way, but an effective leader is going to be able to use these for good outcomes.

- **People Management**

How well are you able to manage the human resources at your disposal? When you see each person as an individual, acknowledging their skills and abilities, you'll find that managing them becomes easier. Learning how to use the personalities of each team member to balance out quirks of another is going to serve you well over the long run. Consider how leaders in your life have balanced out the working environment by teaming up certain individuals to create successful outcomes.

Tips to Bravely Embrace Leadership

Do you find it scary when thinking about being a leader? The chances are if you are in the role of being a leader, whether it is at work or in your personal life, you are in this position for a reason. You have demonstrated the qualities and abilities of an effective leader and sought out to lead others. Below you will find tips that will help you embrace the scary quest of leadership.

- **Realize Your Leadership Gift**

You more than likely have an innate gift for leadership. Look at your strengths that align with the above-mentioned skills of effective leaders. How do these intertwine? Consider your personality, your skills, your abilities, and your way with people. Embrace the gifts that you have within you to effectively lead others to successful outcomes.

- **Immerse Yourself in Learning and Growth Opportunities**

Remember that learning is a continual activity and this is no different when you are learning to be an effective leader. If you are willing to continue improving and growing, you'll find that others seeks you out to lead. Never stop learning because new ideas and concepts are discovered constantly. When you are leading individuals, understanding the psychology behind each person is important. Keep yourself up-to-date on new trends and attend workshops that teach you how to put them into action.

- **Reach a Breaking Point**

Hitting rock-bottom isn't always a bad thing. If you allow yourself to become broken, you are going to find that your leadership qualities improve. If you are in the position of leading right now, think back to what broke you. Did you have a moment in your life where you decided that you needed to be better? If so, consider that the experience drove you even further than you thought possible.

- **Embrace Opportunities**

Each time an obstacle is thrown into your path, embrace it as an opportunity to grow and learn. If you continually embrace the opportunities thrown your way, you are going to see your leadership grow, experiencing new skills and new ways of life. Each opportunity that is given to you is a chance for you to grow - or perhaps even change direction. Embrace these opportunities and go with the flow.

- **Be Focused on Your Vision**

You have a vision for your life. If you are a leader, you also need to have a vision for your team. Keep your focus on this vision and do not allow yourself to falter. With each opportunity, an obstacle that is thrown your way, look for a chance to grow, realigning your direction with your vision, and moving towards making that vision a reality.

- **Get Inspired**

Inspiration is a form of effective leadership. To be inspirational, you yourself first have to be inspired. Take some time to find what is inspirational, using that as a springboard to inspiring others. When you find yourself feeling less than effective, seek out inspiration to spark that fire and get you going again. Do not allow yourself to give up, because when you give up you are letting your team down.

- **Speak Up Often**

When you see injustice in the world, let your voice be heard; there's a good chance someone needs you. As a leader, you should focus not only on your own well-being but also on the well-being of others. This includes people in your community and those sharing the world with you. Make sure that when you disagree with something, speak up and let your opinion be heard. Others may be thinking the same thing but are afraid to say it out loud! You can be their voice.

- **Look at Potential, Not the Past**

In the workplace, it's important to look at the potential in individuals to determine if they have a spot on your team. If you let their past control your decision, you could be missing the opportunity to let someone shine. There are obvious reasons to look at their past (such as a criminal record), but often it's going to benefit you more to see the potential in a person rather than focusing on their past failures.

- **Recognize That You Are Good Enough**

When you recognize that you are good enough to be a leader, you are going to see better outcomes. There is no room in leadership for self-doubt or self-criticism. You need to give yourself the opportunity to embrace who you are and what you can accomplish. If you are down on yourself, you will not accomplish what you are setting out to. If you struggle with self-doubt, remember affirmations are a good way to shove that doubt out of the way.

- **Build on Your Strengths**

You listed your strengths already; build your leadership on those strengths. If you are an effective communicator, use that strength to communicate your vision. Perhaps you are good at negotiating, but your communication is less than stellar, build upon the negotiating qualities that you have to drive your team.

- **Be Courageous**

Leading requires courage. Courage comes from belief in yourself and your abilities. Do what you have to so that you can be courageous as you move forward into the future. Each obstacle that appears should be faced fearlessly. Do not worry about what could happen; just embrace the opportunity as it comes. When you do this, you are facing life full of courage.

- **Don't Look Past Yourself for Affirmation**

You do not need somebody else's approval to be effective. You are simply enough the way that you are. If you look for approval from someone else, you are going to be disappointed. The best place to get the approval that you need is by looking in the mirror and repeating the affirmations that we have discussed. Affirmations are vital to your success, and they need to come from within yourself.

- **Embrace the Spotlight**

As a leader, you are going to be in the spotlight regularly. When something good happens, you are going to be singled out – which always feels great. On the other hand, when something bad happens, you are going to be singled out – which is not always so great. Learn to embrace the focus that is going to be placed upon you because once you do that, you are going to find that you deal with the obstacles and the opportunities much more effectively.

- **You Know What You Stand For**

If you do not know what your values are, you are going to in life and in leadership. You need to stick by what you believe and stand up for the injustices that you see throughout the world. Standing firmly on your values is going to bring you far in life, and this is also going to give you the courage to face adversity. When you clearly define what it is you stand for, each obstacle that comes your way will have no effect on you. Instead, you are going to tackle each obstacle head-on.

Leadership can be scary, but when you practice and learn new skills, you find that your leadership is more effective, and you are gaining confidence in this role. Understanding what your superpower is, what type of leader you are, and how these work together is going to keep you on a straight path to success.

Conclusion

Thank you for making it through to the end of Mindset. You are on your way to unlocking the power of positive thinking and skyrocketing your confidence, success, self-discipline, productivity, focus, self-esteem, mental toughness, social intelligence, and leadership skills. It has been a joy writing this book; I hope it was informative, providing you with all the tools you need to achieve your goals - whatever they may be.

The next step is to work on positive thinking:

- Take responsibility for your present and your future
- Learn and practice living each day with joy
- Practice self-compassion and learn to control your thoughts
- Be in control of your own life and boost your confidence
- Understand who you are and accept responsibility for that person
- Decide what you want your future to look like
- Begin living life on your own terms
- Set goals for yourself
- Learn to face your fears and take action
- Readjust your thought processes
- View obstacles as opportunities

- Commit to improving yourself in your relationships
- Focus on meditation and improving your concentration
- Make a commitment to beat procrastination and become more productive
- Learn how to use affirmations positively in your life
- Understand the concept of mental toughness and how to practice this skill
- Work to improve your social intelligence as well as your social skills
- Understand how your leadership affects those around you as well are your own destiny.

Finally, if you found this book useful in any way, a review on Amazon is always appreciated! Good luck on the journey ahead; I wish you much success in life.

Part 2: Self-Talk

The Ultimate Guide to Transforming Negative Thinking into Positive Thinking and Skyrocketing Self-Esteem, Confidence, Productivity, and Mental Toughness, Including 500 Daily Affirmations

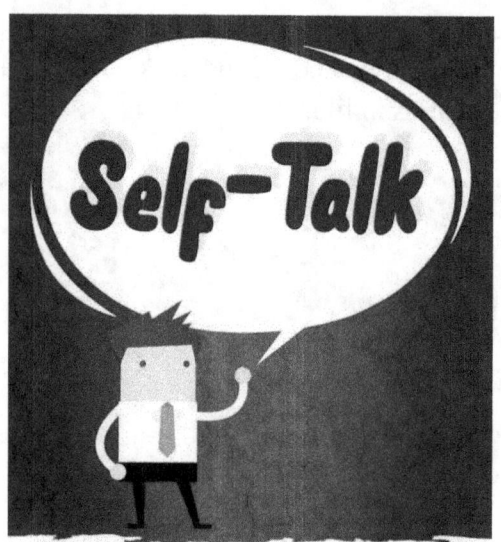

Introduction

All-day long, during every waking moment, our minds are chattering. We think to ourselves, plan out our day, and also criticize ourselves and express our deepest inner beliefs. This inner self-critic is the most devastating of all, worse than any shaming by other people—even though that hurts too. But it is our beliefs about ourselves that cut the deepest wounds.

The beliefs that you hold about your abilities, worth, future, and appearance, among other things, are woven deep into your subconscious. These beliefs can lead to destructive negative self-talk that holds you back from living the most fulfilling and happy life that you can lead. Negative self-talk and the destructive beliefs behind it create bad habits and lead to bad life choices.

That may sound depressing, and many people hold one specific belief that is as destructive as all the others combined—that they cannot change these core inner beliefs that lead to negative self-talk, negative attitudes, and the trap that they create for our lives.

However, we now know that this isn't the case—changing your core beliefs and negative self-talk is something that is in your reach today. And that's what we're going to teach you about in this book.

We will begin by discussing where negative self-talk and the core beliefs that lead to it come from. Then we'll explain the importance of self-love, and how to embrace it without becoming narcissistic.

We'll talk about the importance of a positive attitude, and how to instill it in your children. Then we'll explore the process of recognizing your own negative beliefs and sore points, and how to turn them into strengths. From here, we'll teach you how to eliminate negative thoughts and self-talk, and replace them with a positive can-do attitude. We'll end the book with 500 affirmations that you can use to retrain your mind into a new optimistic, uplifting, and positive self that inspires.

Chapter 1: Where Does Negative Self-Talk Come From?

So, what is self-talk? It's the constant chatter that goes on in our minds. It reflects how we view ourselves and the world around us. You are probably only barely aware of it most of the time, even though it's having a large influence on your own thought patterns and results in life.

Most of the time, self-talk is that "voice in our head." Sometimes it is commenting on regrets from the past, dreams not realized, or mistakes made. Other times, it is talking about the future. Maybe it's telling you that you have dreams, but you aren't going to realize them. All too often, that voice in your head—the voice of your subconscious—is pointing out all of your shortcomings. That inner voice is all too happy to point out the reasons why you aren't going to succeed, or why you can't have a good relationship.

When you're by yourself at home or driving around in your car, the inner voice is probably speaking out loud. Don't worry about it; we all talk to ourselves. But we may differ in the ways that we talk to ourselves. For many of us, our self-talk is negative and brings us down.

Before we can go about changing the negative self-talk and thoughts that plague our lives, we need to understand where they come from in the first place. It turns out that our lives are in part directed by subconscious programs that have been instilled in us since childhood. This is the key to understanding how to change your life. Although we also have a core belief that those programs cannot be changed, just like a computer that can be reprogrammed, our subconscious mind can be reprogrammed as well. In order to do that properly, we need to begin by understanding how it operates in the first place and how those programs were created. This is the topic we are going to investigate in this first chapter.

The Power of Thought

The topic of the subconscious mind is a very large one, indeed. It crosses over many fields of study, including psychoanalysis, cognitive therapy, and neuroscience, among many others. But you don't need to know all the theories about cognitive therapy, or the fundamentals espoused by Carl Jung, in order to have a grasp of how the subconscious programming in your mind works and how to change it. You don't have to be an expert in neuroscience either. To be quite honest, it really doesn't matter how the brain is structured for our purposes.

We begin by making a simple observation about the world. Everything that human beings do or say begins as a thought. It doesn't matter how big or small the task before us is. Landing a man on the moon, or building the Brooklyn Bridge, began as mere thoughts in people's heads. The chair or sofa that you are sitting in as you read this book was also nothing more than a thought at one time. Thought can be said to be one of the main characteristics—if not the central characteristic—that separates humans from other life on earth. We not only have thoughts, but we are able to express them to others and influence the thoughts that others have. This ability to communicate our thoughts is also central to the human experience.

Dogs and cats may have thoughts, but they have a limited ability to communicate them. The same holds true for other animals, and it is our ability to speak and communicate through the written word that has made the difference for human beings.

Thoughts not only shape what human beings can do in the world. They also shape how we view ourselves, our abilities, our appearance, and our relationships with others. Many of us have been trapped by negative thinking in regard to these fundamental thoughts that influence how we feel about ourselves. The impacts of this are wide and far-ranging. Even worse, most people are not even aware of how their negative self-talk is influencing their day-to-day lives and the outcomes that they experience.

So how is the power of negative thoughts—expressed through negative self-talk—realized in our life? If only we could count the ways. Some of the ways that negative self-talk expresses itself include bad or toxic relationships, failure to advance in a career, financial problems, and an inability to lose weight. Negative self-talk can also make us shy and afraid to express ourselves. We become plagued by self-doubt and lack confidence. In truth, the list that I provided right here is merely the beginning of the many things in your life that are influenced by negative self-talk. The negative core beliefs that you have about yourself are expressed daily through negative thoughts. Self-talk is directing the path of your life. But the good news is that you can change it starting right now.

The Subconscious Mind

In order to change the negative self-talk that has governed your life up to this point, you need to understand where it came from in the first place. In practice, it comes from the subconscious mind. The subconscious mind actually isn't as mysterious as it's made out to be. In fact, the subconscious mind is pretty dumb. I would equate the subconscious mind to a blank computer that only does what it's programmed to do. So, in order to change our core beliefs about ourselves, and to change our thought patterns, all we need to do is reprogram the subconscious.

Knowing how to reprogram the subconscious is the first step in moving forward and improving your life. But before we get to that, we need to understand where the negative programs came from in the first place.

The Origins of Negative Thoughts

I have a feeling that this part of the book won't be a surprise to anyone. The negative thoughts that you experience every single day are not real. They were programmed into your mind years—and even decades—ago. The subconscious mind begins the process of being programmed from the time that we are small infants. Anyone who interacted with you when you were a small child had a big influence on the negative thoughts that you are experiencing today. This begins with imparting a general attitude about life and the world and includes your basic view of yourself.

Obviously, your parents or immediate caregivers had a very large impact on shaping your thoughts. Think about how many parents tell their children things like, "You never do anything right!" Some parents even tell their children things like "You're stupid!" and "You're never going to amount to anything!"

But don't blame your parents. Remember that their minds were programmed too, and this has been going on for countless generations, stretching way back through the past. In many cases, parents don't even realize what they are doing or what kind of attitudes they are imparting to their children. If you had a parent like this, forgive them. They were struggling with the same type of inner negative self-talk that you are.

However, it should be straightforward to recognize that if you keep hearing "You're never going to amount to anything," then you are most likely going to adopt this viewpoint into your own life, and once this happens, you'll be the one saying it—in your own self-talk.

Your parents were not the only ones that were having a major influence in those crucial formative years. During ages 2-6, the subconscious mind is especially vulnerable. At this point, it's still a blank slate that is easily programmed. That makes it vulnerable to interactions with other people.

If you had older siblings, they could have a very dramatic impact on your subconscious programming. It's natural for siblings to be competitive, and when you have an older brother or sister, they might be going out of the way to put you down and instill negative thinking in your mind. Of course, I am not saying that all siblings have relationships like this, but it is quite common and even natural.

The same holds for relationships between children. Some of the cruelest people on the planet are children, who can be very mean to their peers between ages 6-17. The range of cruelties can be quite varied. They can push the idea that you are stupid, ugly, fat, uncoordinated—you name it. Perhaps the greatest cruelty of all is shunning.

In many tribal societies, shunning someone and forcing them to leave the group was one of the most dramatic actions that people could take. This even continued into the world of ancient civilization, where people were forced to move to remote islands, even during Roman times.

But this practice hasn't left us. One of the worst things that can happen to a child is they can live in a world where they have no friends because they have been shunned—in a manner that really isn't very different from what happened in many ancient societies. But unless your parents are able to move you into another school and situation, you're actually forced to live among the people who are rejecting you. This can have devastating and long-lasting impacts.

If your parents hire baby sitters or caregivers, they can also create negative thought-processes in your mind. Again, the baby sitter may not even be aware of what he or she is doing; their mind has also been programmed via the subconscious. But they can make negative statements about the children they care for, and given the fact that the subconscious mind is wide open for programming and easily influenced, any statements about you made by other adults or older children in your life while you were a small child can have a big influence.

Another big influence that is strongest when we are aged 5-10 but can still have an impact through the teen and early adult years, is the thoughts and opinions of teachers. Teachers that are positive and uplifting can have a big influence on a child and the thought patterns that the child has. But the opposite is equally true as well. If a teacher has a negative and abusive relationship with the children in their class, or with a specific child, the negative impact can last a lifetime. Think about the many beliefs that a teacher can impart to their students: *you can't do the math; girls don't study engineering; you're slow; you don't speak very well.* The list goes on, and it's a long one. Again, don't blame the teacher. They were programmed just like anyone else who imparted negative self-views on your life.

This brings us to an interesting psychological phenomenon called projection. When a person suffers from a given malady (usually of an emotional or mental nature), they will accuse others of suffering from it. You can think of people that have negative attitudes about others, especially small children, as engaging in the form of projection. The teacher or parent has a negative self-image, and they project this onto others around them.

Your negative self-programming can be influenced in other ways; sometimes these are indirect. If your parents had a toxic relationship, this could also lead to feelings of self-doubt and low self-esteem. You may have heard your father yelling at your mother telling her she was stupid, or maybe your mother called your father "a no-good bum." A small child hearing these types of interactions is ripe for incorporating these thought patterns into their own programming.

So How Does It Work?

The key to these types of thought patterns being adopted by the subconscious mind is repetition. The more the negative statement is heard, the more the subconscious mind incorporates it and learns it. If the statement is incorporated by strong emotions—then it becomes deeply ingrained in the subconscious. Of course, this is going to be the case if someone you love and admire, especially a respected adult, says negative things about you. A parent who is saying something negative will have the largest impact when you are a small child, but when you become school age and hear negative things from teachers or peers, the emotional impact can be just as strong.

When a message is repeated often, or it's accompanied by strong emotions, our subconscious mind accepts it readily. The ability of the subconscious mind to incorporate a message and use it in its programming is stronger when we are young, but it still has this capacity now.

That message won't just be reflected in our inner voice. The negative thoughts—*I'm stupid, I'm fat, I'm ugly, I can't do anything right*—turn into self-fulfilling prophecies. If you believe you're ugly, you'll avoid talking to that person that you're romantically interested in. Or if you do, your negative self-image will make you shy and awkward, ensuring that the result you expect—that they aren't going to be interested in you—is realized. For some people, over time this leads them to seek out toxic relationships, and they may find themselves stuck in an abusive situation, or in one that is constantly filled with lots of drama. Or maybe you avoid relationships altogether, thinking you're not good enough, and so you drift through life feeling lonely.

In fact, that is one path people with negative self-talk often take. The safe path, where safety is defined as the avoidance of situations that might lead to failure. As a result, you might find that you're leading a mediocre life, in the sense that you're not living up to your potential.

Stability is often elusive for people with negative self-talk. If you aren't involved in abusive relationships, you might find yourself having financial problems. When you sit back and take a look, you'll notice that you're never able to realize your goals. Maybe you can't seem to pay off your debts or you never lose weight. Or you're unable to hold a good job and find yourself bouncing from one place of employment to another, never advancing in your career.

Keep in mind that no one person is likely to experience all of these problems, so you might not see yourself in all of them. But one thing we can be sure of is this. If your mind is governed by negative thought patterns, and you are bombarded daily by your negative self-talk, it's holding you back in many ways. In the next section, we are going to go through an exercise so that you can start to become more consciously aware of your negative self-talk, and recognize the ways that it's holding back progress in your life.

The Blank Slate

When you are born, your subconscious mind is barely forming. It really starts to take root at around age two. When we become capable of language and verbal communication with others, our subconscious mind begins developing at a rapid pace, accepting the programming that is given to it.

I like to think of it as a new computer. When you buy a brand-new computer, it has a nearly empty hard disk that is ready to be filled up with information and programs. It runs at tip-top speed. But the more you use it, the more filled up the hard disk becomes, and that once impressive speed and performance becomes more elusive.

The same thing happens with our subconscious mind. As we get older, it's thoroughly programmed. The negative thoughts and self-talk that we experience are so ingrained that we are hardly aware of it, and it is having a real impact on our lives.

When you have a computer that's been used a lot and the hard drive is almost full, it takes some work to bring it back to peak performance again. The same is true of the subconscious mind. It can be reprogrammed. But it's going to take some work. That means you're going to have to put in a conscious effort on a daily basis to "reprogram" yourself. At first, it's going to seem like you're getting nowhere. It's not going to be easy replacing the negative thoughts and emotions that have been in place for decades. But if you stick with it, I promise you that it can be done. And the results are going to be breathtaking.

The Self-Talk Journal

The first step to solving any problem is to recognize it. With this in mind, I encourage you to get a notebook to use as a self-talk journal. This is an incredibly private thing, and it is up to you if you want to share it. If you want to keep it to yourself, that is perfectly fine as well.

The purpose of this exercise is to start becoming consciously aware of your negative self-talk. You probably have some conscious awareness of it, but we want to explicitly identify it.

There are two different ways that the journal can be organized. The straightforward way is to simply write down the negative thoughts that you have each day. Alternatively, you can create a group of categories. This could be done in a multi-subject notebook, for example. The categories could include things like appearance, weight, relationships, career, and intelligence. At first, you might not be sure what categories to use because you may not have been paying close attention to your negative thought patterns. When you become fully consciously aware of them for the first time, you will begin to notice where your negative self-talk is directed, and then you can pick the areas of your life that are most frequently impacted by these thoughts.

Either way, when you write down a negative thought or self-talk that you're experiencing, think about the opposite thought. You can write your thoughts in two columns, with the negative thought on the left side. Then write down the positive thought across from it on the right-hand side. Alternatively, you can simply list your negative thoughts linearly, and put the positive thought below it. For example, if the negative thought is "I always screw up," you can replace it with "We all make mistakes, and I will learn from my mistakes and do better next time." Another example: if you say "I'm stupid" to yourself, you could write down, "I am smart and capable" for your positive thought.

The point of this exercise is to become aware of the negative thoughts you are experiencing and to begin getting your mind to think in different ways that are positive and optimistic.

When Something Becomes a Program, It's an Automatic Response

The first step in the programming process is to condition your subconscious mind into believing something specific about yourself. It then acts back out on the world, in the form of responses to various situations. One of the responses is the negative self-talk that you continually experience. As a simple example, imagine a teenager seeing someone they are attracted to. If their life is governed by negative thoughts, the first thing that their inner voice might say is "They would never go out with me." This negative self-talk then results in practical consequences, namely not talking to the person and therefore getting the result imagined when thinking this way. A perfect example of a self-fulfilling prophecy.

One way that automatic responses are regulated is in your attitude. You can have an attitude of failure, and not even realize it. The negative self-talk that you experience is a result of your attitude, which in turn, like the self-talk that you experience, has been created by the programs that people have been putting into your life from day one.

A program that directs your subconscious mind and the resulting attitudes and self-talk that you experience every day, can also be influenced by something that happens in your adult life. One single off-hand negative comment can create a new negative program that begins operating in your subconscious. In fact, it's amazing how easily we accept negative statements by people and incorporate them into the programs that run our life. Someone might say something like "Those pants are too tight for you," and it will either create or reinforce a belief that we are overweight. As this new negative program is being created, you'll get that sinking feeling in your chest and stomach immediately when the person says it. Then it creates a negative thought such as *I'm fat,* and this is coupled with an attitude, such as *I can never lose weight.*

This brings us to another point to consider in your exercise with a negative self-talk journal. Look at the types of negative thoughts that your self-talk is describing to you. Think about them and then determine what kind of attitude they represent. Then commit to changing the attitude itself.

The Formation of Habits and Desires

The programming that has shaped your subconscious mind has created a set of automatic responses that we can also call habits. These habits are things that you may only be tangentially aware of—if you are aware of them at all. Maybe you are always late. You might always show up late to meet friends for dinner, or maybe you show up late to work or to meetings. There can be many causes of a habit like this, but if it's a result of negative thought patterns, which often produce depression and apathy, the results of your late behavior will only confirm what you already believe about yourself. Your friends might not invite you out as often, or you might get reprimands from your boss or even lose your job.

Desires are emotions that are at the root of our behaviors. Desire is the energy source for the actions we take in our lives. Positive desires can lead to positive results. For example, you might desire to move into a better neighborhood, but it's more expensive. If you are a person with a positive outlook on life, you'll devise a plan to realize your dream. Maybe you'll take on a second job, or work to get a promotion so that you can increase your salary.

The person whose life is dominated by negative self-talk has desires as well, but their negative self-talk works to dampen the desire so that it cannot provide the energy needed to make something happen. If your psyche is dominated by negative self-talk, when your desire springs to move to a better neighborhood, you'll talk yourself out of it. You'll tell yourself all the reasons why it's impossible. *I can't afford it. I could never afford it. I'll never make enough money to move over there.*

When a program has become deeply ingrained into our subconscious mind, it creates habits, which are a series of automatic behaviors in our lives. It's been said that these habits are like a plane running on autopilot. The plane just flies along and heads to its pre-determined destination. If you've been programmed into negative thinking, you're flying on autopilot, living a life governed by negative habits that prevent you from being completely happy and fulfilled.

External Circumstances Create Negative Thinking: You Have to Change it From Within

As we stated earlier, your subconscious mind was programmed by your early interactions and experiences. These highly formative experiences have become thoroughly ingrained by the time you hit adolescence, although your experiences in adolescence can also strongly shape your internal programs as well. If you have a good experience in your teenage years and early adulthood, it is possible to overcome negative programs and replace them with positive thinking. But for many of us, the negative programs are reinforced.

Bad experiences in adolescence, which is a period of time characterized by extremely high levels of emotion, can strongly ingrain negative emotions and self-talk, essentially making them permanent unless we consciously work to invoke change.

That change has to come from within. You can't change by blaming your parents, your teachers, or childhood friends. You can't change by blaming bad experiences or outcomes. You have to take charge of your own life and the results that come with it. This is the meaning of "personal responsibility."

Simple Ways to Reprogram Your Thought Processes and Feelings

If you feel negative all the time, for most people, this is going to be reflected in their behavior. Some people are able to put a happy face over their negative self-image, but for most of us, it's going to carry forward into our behavior. A person that feels bad about themselves will often carry themselves in a negative way. They won't look people in the eye or smile. They may have a slouched posture. They will speak in a low voice, without enthusiasm. They'll feel tired all the time.

What if this person (maybe it is you) simply approached the world differently? The subconscious mind has been programmed, and it controls us if we let it do so. But you don't have to let it control you. Try walking out the door with an erect posture and a smile. Make an effort to look people in the eye, and speak with some enthusiasm.

Changing Your Habits

One of the first ways you can start eliminating negative self-talk is to change the habits that result from it. The first step is to identify all of your bad habits that arise from your negative attitudes, and the negative self-talk that results from those attitudes. At first, it is going to seem artificial, but you can make a lot of progress by forcing yourself to adopt habits that are associated with the opposite, positive attitude. Maybe you are late to work all the time because you have an attitude of failure. Sure, you can and should work on the attitude of failure, but something that will start to reverse it quickly at the subconscious level, is simply arriving to work early each day. Start acting as if you have the enthusiasm to go wherever you need to go so that you switch from being the person who is always ten minutes late to the person who is five minutes early.

The fact is that programs in our subconscious mind work in both directions. So, you can become conditioned to think a certain way, and then this thinking process and point of view becomes adopted by your subconscious mind. Then it acts outward, creating negative thought patterns and self-talk, and the negative habits and behaviors that come with it. For example, if you have a poverty mindset, the simple reality is that you are going to manifest a poverty cycle. You are going to hear constant mind chatter that only people who are connected and lucky make money, and you're never going to get out of the situation that you are in. Constantly hearing that kind of talk will put you in a trap, because you are going to act in ways that are consistent with the mindset. You won't be looking for any ways to get out of your current work situation, to improve your pay, upgrade your skillset, or start a business. Instead, you will find ways to cast blame on others and external circumstances.

But the good news is that we can go the other way, and reprogram our subconscious using our own active efforts. In your childhood, the programming of your subconscious was set by the impressions, thoughts, and words of others. It still is, to some extent, and a negative remark from a loved one or a colleague at work can reinforce the negative programs that are already operating in your psyche.

However, we can start "rewriting" these programs ourselves, by consciously saying thoughts that we want to manifest (affirmations) and by changing our habits using conscious effort.

Maybe in the mornings, you wake up depressed, not wanting to face another day. Your habit may be to sleep until the very last moment when you have to get up, and then slowly get ready to drag yourself to work.

Try something different over the next week. If the weather is good, get up 30 minutes early instead of sleeping in, and go outside for a brisk walk. Put a smile on your face and make it a point to enjoy the walk. If you encounter others along the way, smile and say hello in a friendly manner, and be open to stopping and chatting with them for a minute and making new friends.

Do this for an entire week, and I will tell you with absolute certainty that you are going to find that you feel a lot better about your life. This one simple act by itself might start changing some of that negative self-talk that you are experiencing day-in and day-out.

Think of other behaviors that you can change that are related to your negative programs. In order to do this, you need to write down a list of the major areas in your life where you are feeling the most negativity.

Do you have a large debt to pay off? A student loan or credit card bills? Unfortunately, too many of us do these days. Maybe you've only been making the minimum payments. It will be difficult for many people to do, but put a small amount of money aside each month in order to increase your payments. Even if it's just $20, it will help, but if you can put $50 or $100 aside, that is even better. That way, you are not going to just be paying the minimum and taking eons of time to pay off the bill. I assure you that the first time that you pay that extra $20, by changing your action through conscious effort, you are going to change the way you feel about your life instantly. You are literally going to feel a weight lifting off your shoulders the first time that extra payment is made.

You can start making small changes like this throughout your life and experience the positive results—but it's going to be important that you commit to the changes. When you do, you're going to find that by working inward, using the conscious mind to force changes in your behavior, that you are going to start seeing changes in the self-talk that has been causing you problems and holding you back.

Negative Emotions are Normal

Everyone has negative emotions from time to time, and the emotions we experience are not the problem. It's the way that we *respond* to the emotions that is the root of the problem.

Think about the negative emotions you would feel if you knocked over a glass vase, and it breaks. You could say to yourself "I can't do anything right," or you can clean up the mess and tell yourself "I'll be more careful next time." If you've broken the glass vase in someone else's home or at work, acknowledge the mistake and offer to pay for it, and move on.

Naturally, you are going to feel negative about breaking something, or doing something wrong, or saying something hurtful to a loved one. But you can choose to view the event as a learning experience and move on, or you can dwell on it and use negative self-talk to keep focusing on it and grow it into a large problem, that ends up damaging your self-esteem.

Negative self-talk can be viewed as *destructive* self-talk because it gets in the way of your goals and ambitions. This is different from constructive criticism, which acknowledges a mistake and then seeks to find a way to make something good come from the mistake. So, it doesn't get in the way of progress, it helps you get there.

Affirmations

Remember that a habit and an attitude—the programming of our subconscious mind—is created by repetition and/or strong emotions. The good news is that we can do the reverse. You can reprogram your subconscious mind by using affirmations. Other people were doing the programming when you were growing up. Now it's your turn to do the programming and direct your own outcomes. Affirmations will work best when combined with habit changes.

Remember, the subconscious mind is dumb. It's like a computer that just does what it's programmed to do. While it takes some time and effort, we can readjust the subconscious mind from the top down. So, we are going to put in an effort to reprogram the mind, and we can use affirmations to fill our mind with the positive thoughts that we want to have. So, in short, this is a way to reprogram the subconscious mind using statements that we *want* to believe. These are positive and uplifting statements that are known as "affirmations."

To get you started, we have included 500 affirmations at the end of the book. That is just for starters. If you need affirmations for a specific area of your life, you can look online to find more. But after reading some affirmations, it shouldn't be too difficult to come up with your own. You can even use your negative self-talk to come up with affirmations to replace it. Remember, I suggested that in your journal you write down the positive thought that is the opposite of the negative self-talk you are troubled by.

When using affirmations, the trick is a lot of repetition. Studies show that when you learn something, the way you learn it is by doing it over and over. When you were in school, this is how you passed your exams. I suspect that most people learn what they need to learn for an exam by repeating it in their head over and over again. This helps move the fact—or whatever you are trying to learn—into the memory banks of your brain, and into the realm of the subconscious. That way, it can be automatically recalled. Your brain literally changes its structure in order to encode the new information.

Just think about that last statement for a little bit. Your brain was actually structured as you were growing up by the negative ideas that people were feeding your mind. This is why the negative programs run so efficiently today. It is as if they changed the hardware *and* the software.

Repetition is one of the most effective ways to do this, but strong emotion can help drive it down with a single occurrence. This is another thing that has been demonstrated in many studies. People will often remember traumatic events very well because the force of the emotion etches it into memory. The same thing happens when someone makes a negative comment about you if you are already in a position of having negative thought processes. If they say something implying that you are not good enough, are incompetent, are fat, ugly, or whatever the case may be—the emotional response to the comment will ensure that the thought the other person is conveying gets incorporated into your subconscious mind.

It may be difficult to replicate that kind of emotional response, but we do have the power to implement a program of repetition.

The power of repetition isn't just reflected in studying. It shows what it can do when people learn a new skill. Think of a professional tennis player. If they had to think about all the steps they use to locate and hit a tennis ball coming at them at high speed, they wouldn't possibly be able to do it. The conscious mind simply isn't capable of analyzing the situation and directing your limbs and muscles to respond appropriately in a short enough amount of time.

The way that it is done is through the subconscious. By using repetition over the course of years—what we commonly call "practice" when considering the acquisition of the skill of some type—the movements required are driven into the subconscious mind where they become automatic programs, just like the programs that direct our negative self-talk.

Reprogramming the Subconscious Mind

When it comes to replacing negative self-talk with positive thoughts, the way to start getting this done is to engage in the repetition of positive affirmations three times a day or more. You should keep the number of affirmations to a minimum. Start off by identifying an area of your life that you want to work on first. Then pick out three to five affirmations related to this topic and repeatedly say the affirmations to yourself during three daily meditation sessions. You should repeat each affirmation about five times per session. Say them slowly and methodically so that you aren't rushing through it.

At first, you aren't going to believe what you are saying. But as we've said before, the subconscious mind is a dumb receptacle. So, if you keep telling it what you want to believe, the subconscious mind is going to accept it, and incorporate the statements into its own programs. Once this happens, you will start to see your negative self-talk begin to change. If you combine this process with the use of habits, the changes you see will happen more rapidly and will be stronger.

Chapter 2: Why Self-Love Matters

Self-love is not about narcissism. We are talking about a perfectly normal level of self-esteem. But why is this important? I'm sure that you realize that with good self-esteem, you would feel better about yourself. But it goes way beyond that. Replacing the negative self-talk that you constantly experience with healthy and positive thoughts will actually change the direction of your life. You probably don't realize it, but the negative self-talk that you experience is actually holding back your potential for success. This cuts across all aspects of life. In other words, negative self-talk not only prevents you from having career success, but it will also inhibit your ability to get ahead financially. It's either going to prevent you from getting in relationships or ensure that you are trapped in bad and abusive relationships. Of course, I'm not saying this is going to happen to everyone, but on some level we are all affected by negative self-talk, which plagues our lives and sets limits on what we can do.

The reason is that negative self-talk creates a reinforcement mechanism that solidifies the negative beliefs that we have about ourselves. Those negative beliefs constrain the actions that we take in the real world. They also conspire to attract negative things into our lives. When you give negative thoughts energy, you are going to attract negative energy in return. This negative energy can take many forms. It might be in the form of bad people that are coming into your life. Or it might be in the form of bad outcomes and results. This is why self-love matters. Self-love is going to enable you to direct positive energy, instead of negative energy. And what that's going to do for you, besides making you feel better, is you are going to start seeing better results in your life.

How and Why Negative Self-Talk Manifests in Negative Results

Most of us aren't even fully conscious of the negative self-talk that we are experiencing every single day. And so, it's not surprising that we fail to make the connection between negative self-talk and the results this brings to our lives. In fact, we use it to justify the negative thoughts that continually run through our brains. Many people misinterpret the thoughts that they are experiencing, believing that they reflect the outcomes in their life, rather than the other way around. Now this isn't to say that you will never have a negative experience that leads to negative thought processes. That certainly does happen at times. But for those of us who are living a life that is dominated by negative self-talk, it's actually the other way around.

 So, what happens is: a negative experience or comment creates a belief system that leads to negative thoughts. The negative thoughts impact our actions in the present-day. This could have long-lasting implications. Suppose that you were a 12-year-old girl with an interest in mathematics and science. If the teacher that you looked up to came and told you that as a girl you could not do mathematics, that could cause a lot of self-doubts. Maybe the teacher is a little bit coy about their belief, so they don't come out and say it exactly like that. In fact, if they did, it might cause you to get angry at them and become determined to overcome the prejudice against you. So, what if instead they just simply told you that you didn't have the acumen required for a career in math and science? That is more likely to be incorporated into your psyche as a negative belief system. And this will have a direct impact on the future course of your life. After you come to believe that you are not good at math, you will then probably avoid taking more math and science courses in your schooling. And as a result, you will end up pursuing a totally different career path than you otherwise would have.

There are many other ways that negative comments can have an impact that goes well beyond simple negative thoughts. If someone is led to believe that they're ugly or undesirable as a partner, their heads will be full of negative thoughts about this on a daily basis. The negative thoughts will lead to depression and withdrawal. This can manifest in many ways, including shyness or an inability to speak clearly, which will actually confirm the perception. In other words, if you start acting shy and awkward, then people are not going to want to socialize with you. You will see the belief that you're not suitable as a romantic partner confirmed in the external world, and this will only strengthen the programs that are going on inside your mind.

So that is one example of what we might classify as a "self-fulfilling prophecy." There are many others. If you are young and have a perception that you're overweight, there is a good chance that you're going to end up as overweight later on in adulthood. Another self-fulfilling prophecy that is very common as a result of negative thought processes is financial troubles. People who have negative feelings about money or have a negative view about their ability to earn money, often find themselves later on in a state of just getting by—if not in outright poverty.

Negative self-talk also has an unfortunate effect on your health. Think about it. If you have negative emotions about many aspects of your life—if not all aspects of your life—that is going to heighten the stress and anxiety that you feel every single day. This is going to cause many physical symptoms, and the problem with the symptoms is that they are going to be general and vague. Many people will attribute them to working too much or simply due to aging. So, for example, you are probably going to suffer from a bit of insomnia. You might also experience a lot of body pains. It won't surprise you to learn that many people that suffer from negative thought processes and negative self-talk tend to be hypochondriacs. The constant stress and anxiety that is experienced can lead to symptoms such as chest pain or stomach pain. In fact, in some cases, the perceptions of pain can actually manifest as a real illness. If the person is lucky, they will only have headaches and possibly a stomach ulcer. While recent research has linked stomach ulcers to a type of bacteria, it still remains true that if you are under constant stress, and your life is filled with anxiety, that you are more likely to get a stomach ulcer.

Negative self-talk can cause many other health problems. It's possible to experience digestive problems such as diarrhea and to suffer from muscle tension and pain. In a worst-case scenario, the increased levels of stress combined with the lack of sleep can lead to an increased rate of illnesses.

Sadly, these problems seem to be only getting worse. The reason is that the rapid development of technology is causing some people to become more isolated. Social isolation can often make the problem worse. If you become withdrawn and have less social contact, that gives more time for your mind to fill itself with negative thoughts. This can further deepen the problem. If you are someone who has negative thought processes about your social worth, and then you're sitting at home having more thoughts and self-talk related to this topic, it might make you far less likely to venture out and make new friends.

The Reality Distortion Field

Someone once said that Steve Jobs created a reality distortion field. This was a comment made in relation to the way people became fanatical about Apple products. If your mind is filled with negative self-talk, you are creating your own reality distortion field. But unlike the reality distortion field associated with Apple products, the reality distortion field created by negative self-talk is going to be uniformly negative. This can lead to further perception problems and even serious mental health problems like depression. It's certainly going to lead to increased anxiety, especially in social situations.

When you are suffering from the reality distortion field created by negative thought processes, something that's going to happen is you're going to blow things way out of proportion. This can create conflict with people around you. At work, you might be known as someone who is "touchy." The negative thought processes that you continually experience are going to cause your self-esteem to plummet. And so, if anyone makes an offhand remark, you are more likely than the average person to interpret it in a negative way. Unfortunately, this is often going to happen even when the remark is objectively not negative. So, other people are going to start feeling guarded around you. This creates a snowball effect that leads to more negative thoughts in your mind, and the external reality created by your misperception only confirms the negative thoughts, like a self-reinforcement mechanism.

Another side effect caused by this negative reality distortion field is that you're going to be constantly playing the blame game. This can happen on two levels. First off, since you have a negative attitude about yourself, you are going to be blaming yourself for many of the actions that happen in your life. But in this case, we are talking about blaming yourself when you were not at fault. However, sometimes, you are also going to be blaming other people for your problems. And in this situation, the reality is that in fact you are the cause of the problems. We will talk about the blame game in a later chapter in more detail.

The reality distortion field caused by negative thought processes and self-talk often manifests itself in a belief system where your mind always seems to involve you in everything. The fact is, many things happen that seem to be directly connected to us, and sometimes people take actions that appear negative, but they really have nothing to do with us at all. But if you are trapped in the world of negative self-talk, you are more likely than not to interpret nearly every action and reaction in personal terms. Maybe someday a colleague shows up to work in a bad mood because she had a fight with her husband, and when you pass her in the hallway she isn't very enthusiastic about seeing you. Somebody with a healthy attitude might recognize that maybe she was having a bad day, and that's how they would interpret the interaction. But if you are trapped in a world of negative thought processes, you interpret everything in terms of you. So, in the same interaction, you would take it personally if the woman was not very friendly as she passed. You would be wondering what you did to upset her. Or even worse, you might use it as an excuse to reinforce your belief that you're not a worthy person.

Another impact of the reality distortion field created by negative thought processes is that people who have this problem will extend their negative beliefs to all aspects of life. For example, let's say that you are playing basketball with some friends, and you keep messing up, so your teammates get that little bit upset. Of course, from an objective perspective, most people will recognize that such events have very little significance. Once the game is over, your friends will completely forget what happened and move on. But if you're suffering from low self-esteem caused by negative self-talk, it's going to stick with you and you are going to use it as an example that supposedly illustrates your worth as a person in general. The incident will reinforce your negative beliefs about yourself and probably enhance depressive feelings.

Another very common way of negatively interpreting the world is known by psychologists as filtering. In any given situation, there are usually positive and negative things that happen. In order to objectively evaluate the situation, you would weigh the good and the bad and take the average. But if your life has been programmed so much that you're dominated by negative thought processes all the time, you filter out any positive things that happened. In fact, you may be filtering all day long, which means that every day, you will only see the negative aspects of what happened. When you only see the negative aspects of the events that happen in your life, it reinforces the negative views that you already had. And so, it will strengthen the negative self-talk that you are experiencing. Also, it's important to note that failing to see the good side of every event that happens will lead you to experience more negative results in the future.

Another problem that people have is called polarized or black-and-white thinking. In this case, you look at every action that you take in black-and-white terms. So, in other words, you are either perfect or are you are a failure. The problem with this is that striving for perfection is something that's virtually impossible. And since you cannot be perfect in every interaction, this will translate into viewing everything as a complete failure. Of course, most things that happened in life are not either perfection or failure. They are usually somewhere in the middle, and maybe weighted a little bit one way or the other. But by seeing everything as a failure, this only serves to reinforce the negative thought processes that are causing you to think this way in the first place. So almost every event that you experience is going to confirm the perception that you're not quite adequate, leading you to feel even more low self-esteem.

Another problem that often comes out of the reality distortion field of negative thought processes is what's called the control fallacy. This can manifest in one of two ways. The first way this can manifest is in a false belief that you have more control over outcomes and the way people behave than you actually do. Since people are often going to act in ways that you don't like, it's going to give the illusion that you are causing a lot of negative events when in reality you have nothing to do with it.

When it comes to people with negative thought processes, however, there is a more common way that the control fallacy manifests. This is in the belief that you have no control whatsoever over your life. That is, you believe that everything is working against you or everything is due to luck. You begin to see yourself as a victim in life. Someone who sees themselves as a victim is someone who's not going to take control of their life and institute changes that would be beneficial.

So, I want to take a step back at this time and congratulate you on reading this book. By reading this book, you are actually taking action. It may only be the first step on your journey, but taking that first step is a very important way to move forward. Simply by becoming more informed, you are getting away from the victim mentality.

Now, let's move onto another common thought process that is often found among people with negative self-talk. This is using the word "should," and the phrase "should have" far too often. Now, all of us have a list of things that we "should" do in order to improve ourselves. But if you start finding yourself with a big self-improvement "should" list, that can be an indication that you have a reality distortion field that isn't healthy. Perhaps the worst manifestation of this is living in the past and filling your thought processes with "should have." It's normal to have regrets. But it's not normal to continually live in the past. Yes, we all have things that we should have done in the past. But if you are continually focused on it, that indicates you need to take a step back. Learn your lessons from the past without dwelling on them.

Finally, we will end this section with one more aspect of distorted thinking that psychologists have focused on. This is called global labeling. We all fail at some task or in a relationship at some point. But what happens when a person is suffering from global labeling is that they generalize their failure in order to characterize their entire personality. The characteristic phrase associated with this outlook is "I'm such a loser." So, if the person makes a mistake—no matter how minor—they start feeling bad about themselves. But instead of just learning from the mistake and moving on, they generalize the feeling from the mistake into a general sense of low self-esteem and unworthiness.

Learned Helplessness

One of the main impacts of negative self-talk is creating boundaries for ourselves. As we have mentioned, this negative programming usually results from the negative thought processes that others have put into our subconscious minds over the years—stretching way back into our childhoods. This relates to a concept called self-efficacy, which is your ability to achieve goals.

When you are suffering from learned helplessness, you have a low amount of self-efficacy because you put up artificial obstacles subconsciously. This happens because you perceive a lack of control over your life.

Let's use the negative statement "I'm so stupid" as an example. Often, misguided parents will tell their kids they are stupid when they make a mistake. They don't do it because they really believe their children are stupid (at least most of the time). They have a misguided belief that by calling their children stupid, or pointing out that they are acting stupid in a given situation, they are going to motivate the child into behaving better in the future. Instead, what happens is the child incorporates the dysfunctional belief that they are stupid. Over the years, this will be reinforced.

It will start to set limits in the real world as well. If you start believing that you are stupid on a subconscious level, you are going to start feeling as though taking action, in some ways, is futile. So, you won't study as hard in school as you would have otherwise. As a result, you get mediocre grades—confirming the perception that you are in fact, stupid.

You will also fail to take action. Maybe by the time you go to work, the belief is thoroughly ingrained in your psyche. So, if you believe that your opinion and insights are not going to be valued, then you might doubt the value of them yourself. In meetings at work, you may remain quiet and aloof, and this might create a perception among others that in fact, you're not very capable. Doing the minimum to get by, since you have a total lack of belief in yourself, you might feel as though you can do no more. This will relegate you to the bottom rungs, and you'll never improve your situation.

This is an example of how learned helplessness can manifest many years down the road. This is but one example of a poverty mentality. People can have a poverty mentality for many different reasons, but in all cases, the poverty mentality is something that is going to hold people back from living up to their fullest potential. The poverty mentality is characterized by many of the distorted thought processes discussed in the last section. For example, if you have a poverty mentality, one thing you are going to do is blame others for your situation. You will also suffer from a mentality dominated by the control fallacy, believing that others (or "luck") are controlling your fate, rather than facing the reality that you control your own fate.

When you believe that you have no control over the situations that you find yourself in, then you are not going to take any action to get out of them. Your overall productivity and growth will suffer as a result. You are going to go through your life feeling resentful and bitter.

So how do you overcome learned helplessness? The first thing is to identify the limiting beliefs that are showing up in your life as a result of your negative thought processes. This is going to include many of the problems that we discussed in the previous section.

Start by looking at a negative experience after it happens and see how you attribute the cause. For example, you might make a mistake at work that leads to your boss reprimanding you. You might respond in this way:

"I am not good at anything I do."

But maybe there are other causes that led to the problem. Take a look at the situation and see if there are other explanations. Maybe you didn't sleep well the night before, or maybe a co-w0rker gave you incorrect information. The details of what you observe about the situation are less important than avoiding generalizing. This is one of the most insidious problems that arises from negative self-talk. Look at the statement above—it's generalized a minor mishap at work into something that describes your overall capabilities and worth as a person.

So, start by limiting negative events to the situation at hand. Sometimes we just have to accept that we made a mistake, but we also need to recognize that we can learn from the mistake and do better next time. And more importantly, we need to recognize that one mistake doesn't mean that we are a bad person in general.

One of the most negative thought processes that can arise from learned helplessness is a belief that you can't change. If you are experiencing learned helplessness, there is no doubt that this belief is manifesting itself in many negative thought patterns and self-talk that is ruling your daily life. It can be said to be a feeling that you are trapped by your negative situation. This is the victim mentality that many people are trapped in today. You can start improving your life very rapidly by dropping the victim mentality and thinking in terms of someone who is in control of their life. The first step in that journey is to reframe your thoughts.

Reframing Your Thoughts

One of the central ways that you can overcome negative self-talk is by reframing your thoughts. This requires you to do a little bit of analysis and turn your negatives into positives. One way is to use the ABCDE method that was developed by psychologist Martin Seligman, who was inspired by the ABC Model first developed by Albert Ellis. We are going to describe our own version of it.

The ABCDE method can be framed in the following way:

- A is for Adversity. We all experience adversity in our lives. The first step is to describe the adverse situation that happened, which led you to have negative thoughts about yourself.

- B is for Beliefs. Look for the beliefs that are determining how you have interpreted the event. When you start using these exercises, these will be the automatic beliefs that you have created in your subconscious mind as a result of years of negative programming.
- C is for Consequences. What are the consequences of your negative beliefs? In particular, look for the feelings you experience and also actions that you take, as a result of the beliefs that you connect to the adverse event.
- D is for Dispute. That is, look at any of the beliefs that you have connected to the situation and dispute those that are not objectively valid. Replace your inappropriate interpretations and actions that result from the event with better feelings and actions.
- E is for Energy. Focus on the feelings that you get by responding to the situation in a positive and appropriate way.

Adopt an Attitude of Being in Control

Of course, fate does play some role in our lives. You could have been born in poverty on some remote island. But you weren't, and we have to deal with the here and now and not hypotheticals. The fact is this: you have a lot of control over your own life and your fate. Start taking an attitude of control and watch your life improve as a result.

Being in control doesn't necessarily mean that you are going to be able to control the outcome of every situation, or that you can control what comes in and out of your life. What you definitely have control over is the way that you react to different situations. So, you can start there.

Second, although we can't control everything, the fact is that we actually do have a huge amount of control over major aspects of our lives. That doesn't mean we have complete control. Is everyone going to get into Harvard University? Of course not. But you can still get a good college education, and if you study hard, you will come out as educated as someone from Harvard and you will do just as well in the workplace.

Try setting some small goals and working to realize them. Achieving small goals is one way to start building self-confidence. When you start to see that you are able to set goals and achieve them, then you will start feeling more like you are in control of your own life. You will also begin to experience more positive self-talk in response to the increased levels of self-confidence, and your belief systems will begin to change.

Categorizing Your Negative Self-Talk

In the first chapter, we suggested that you keep a self-talk journal. Now that you have become aware of learned helplessness and the many different ways that your thought patterns can be dysfunctional in the reality distortion field, go back and take a closer look at your negative self-talk. See if you can categorize each of your thoughts in a particular manner. For example, is a thought representing black and white thinking? Or are you engaging in filtering? Sometimes a thought is going to fit more than one category, but you can try to list them as best you can. If a particular thought fits more in one category than another, then classify it with the one that best describes it. You can also count the number of times that you are having thoughts of a specific type and then add them up to see what percentage is the largest among the many possibilities.

This will help you understand your negative thought processes more clearly, and possibly help you to identify which characteristics of the reality distortion field best describe your overall thought process. For example, some people are going to find that they are suffering from black & white thinking. This will help them to develop an effective strategy to overcome their negative self-talk.

Turn Negative Thoughts into Positive Thoughts

Earlier, you wrote down a positive thought that was the opposite of a negative thought in your journal. Start doing this on an active basis. This is going to require developing your ability to recognize negative self-talk as it happens.

There are four key phrases that are associated with negative self-talk in terms of reality distortion and learned helplessness. These are:

- "I always …"
- "I can't …"
- "I never …"
- "I am …"

These phrases describe absolute statements. It is important to pick up when they appear in your inner dialogue and then actively replace them with a more appropriate thought.

For example, you can replace: "I never do anything right," with "I made a mistake in this situation, but I will do better next time." If you can start identifying and correcting statements that occur in your inner chatter, which involve these types of absolute qualifiers, you will go a long way to improving your negative self-talk.

The Importance of Raising Children with a Positive Attitude

As you can see from what we are discussing so far, it's going to be a difficult road to recovery once you've been trapped by the negative thought processes that plague many people's lives, especially when you reach adulthood. This is why it's important to raise children that have a positive self-image.

Of course, there is always a danger of creating a little narcissist. So, the goal should be to have children that have positive feelings of self-esteem, but not inflated views of themselves or their abilities. Sadly, there has been a little too much of the latter going around in recent decades. We certainly want children to feel good about themselves and to believe that they can achieve their goals if they set their minds to them, but not everyone is going to "save the world." So, it is important to have your children learn positive thought patterns that are realistic.

We certainly don't want to have children that adopt an attitude of learned helplessness. Your children are not victims, so make sure that they don't fall into that trap. When you spot your children adopting an attitude of learned helplessness, you can step them through the ABCDE method, so that they can learn to identify feelings of learned helplessness themselves and then work their way through the thought processes that are behind it and overcome them.

Second, since you are aware of the patterns of negative thinking that manifest in ways such as black and white thinking, generalization, and so forth, learn to recognize these destructive thought patterns in your children and then help them to get a more realistic picture of reality. So, if your child generalizes—that is, they make a mistake and then generalize it by thinking that as a result they are a "total loser" or "stupid"—help them to differentiate between the single act itself and their worth as an individual.

By starting to foster positive thinking while they are young, you can help your children build up a reserve of resilience. All of us are going to experience adversity throughout our lives, which is going to cause us to doubt ourselves. But if we have a strong foundation to lean on, then we won't give in to negative thought processes and then suffer the wide-reaching consequences of these.

If you are reading this book and suffering from negative self-talk yourself, you may have unconsciously imparted some of those thought patterns to your children. In fact, this has been going on for time immemorial, and it's the reason that these types of thought patterns are here now. They didn't materialize out of thin air, and you may have gotten your own negative self-talk from programs your own parents instilled in you during your childhood.

So now is your chance to break the cycle. Remember that you are not going to be the only influence in your child's life, and there are going to be some things that you cannot control. The only thing you can do is build a foundation for your child that they can call upon when confronted by negativity from teachers or peers. If you have more than one child, you can help the situation because many of us also get a lot of negative thought patterns and beliefs about ourselves from interactions with our siblings.

Simply getting rid of or preventing the victim mentality can go a long way to ensuring the success of your child as they grow up. So many people in today's world are held back as a result of this outlook.

There are some simple, practical steps you can take to help your children develop a habit of positive self-talk. Develop shortlists of affirmations for them to say. You can also help your children come up with their own positive affirmations.

Teach your children about the benefits of positive self-talk, and explain the problems with negative self-talk. As your children get older, these discussions can become more in-depth. You can also explain to them how to change a negative thought into a positive thought. Use specific examples that are directly relevant to their lives.

One important thought pattern that you want to get out of your child's mind is the belief that things happen because of luck. This type of thought needs to be replaced by the recognition that things happen as a result of the actions we take in our lives beforehand. So, if a child scores high on an exam, is that due to luck? Some children may think so, but the reality is that scoring high on an exam is due to studying hard in 99/100 cases. So, you might ask your child why they did good on an exam and have them explain in detail, and if they answer that it was due to "luck," you can offer them guidance in order to reframe this thought.

As another example, a child may have been rejected by a crush. You can help them to see that this is an isolated situation and that being rejected by someone they are attracted to does not generalize into negative subjective statements—such as that they are "ugly" or "undesirable." Help them to understand that there may be specific reasons for the rejection that might not even have anything to do with them, such as the love interest already being involved with someone else.

For smaller children, you can help them learn the power of positive thinking by making crafts that have positive thoughts on them. They can use these before going to school to start their day with a positive mindset.

Getting nervous in challenging, difficult, and new situations is one of the greatest difficulties that children will face. You can help them overcome this by teaching them positive thoughts to say to themselves when they recognize that they feel nervous.

You will also want to teach your children to avoid thinking in terms of regret. Imagine the lifetime of pain that they will avoid if they learn this skill early on. Teach them that the way to approach major mistakes that they made in the past is to learn what the mistake was, and avoid making it again in the future. Teach them that they should not dwell on past mistakes and keep replaying them in their heads.

You should also teach your children to recognize the absolutes that characterize negative thinking. If you remember, these included the phrases, "I never …", "I am …", "I can't …", and "I always …." Whenever a child uses these phrases in their language, this is something that should be addressed right away. These types of absolute statements characterize the type of thinking that we discussed in the "reality distortion field" section. Examine each statement of this type and then correct it, or should I say correct the misperception that is present in the statement.

For example, any absolute statement like "I never …" should be easily replaced by a positive thought process. We all know that the world is not framed in absolute terms. But even us adults who are trapped by negative self-talk and negative thought processes often engage in these types of statements without realizing how unrealistic they are. So, one thing that's important to take care of is yourself. Before you get your children on a correct path to thinking positive thoughts, it's important that you are able to think in a correct manner first.

Another thing you need to instill in your children is how to recognize the context of a situation. For example, help them to recognize that people often say bad things that they don't really mean. A child may say a nasty comment to another child when they're upset about something else; and in fact, you probably realize that this can happen among adults as well. So, you should develop this skill on your own, and that will make it easier to teach your children how to interpret their interactions with others properly. Think back to the earlier example of someone who appeared unfriendly when greeting you at work. Remember it was suggested that maybe that person was having problems at home? The same thing may be influencing a situation involving your child. A peer on a sports team or at school could be having a bad day for some reason or another. Maybe they have problems at home, or a girl they are interested in rejected them, or they had a bad result on an exam. And so, they take this out on your child. Maybe you can discuss this with your child and ask them if they know of anything that might have happened to the other child to cause them to act in a negative way. The key point of this exercise is for your child to recognize that not everything is about them. Some people will react in a negative manner when the root cause is completely unrelated to you, and so you should not take the events as a reason to generate more negative thoughts about yourself.

Another thing that's important to deal with when it comes to children, is helping them to recognize that there is always another day. Children live more in the here and now than adults do. As a result of this, they are more likely to take an individual result or event far more seriously. In the heat of the moment, children may find it difficult to realize that there are going to be many more opportunities to redo the situation. For example, if they are an athlete, it may be hard for them to conceptualize the fact that they are going to have many seasons and games ahead of them, within which they can strive to perform far better than they did during the current game or practice that is causing them angst. So, part of your job as a parent is to help them recognize that today's game is not going to be the end of their story. It's just one event among many throughout their lives.

You can also take any negative situation and get the child to refocus. That is, help them to recognize the positives that occurred in this situation. If you remember when we discussed the reality distortion field, one of the dysfunctional methods of thinking that people who are trapped by negative self-talk engage in, is looking at things in a black-and-white fashion. Children are more likely than adults to look at situations in black-and-white terms. One of the things you can do, is to help them see that there are never situations that are entirely black-and-white. As part of this exercise, you can help them to recognize that the experience that they are currently seeing in black-and-white terms is actually full of shades of gray. That way, they can learn to pick out the positives from any situation and start learning to focus on those instead.

And of course, you need to help your child to learn that they are not a bad person or a failure if they recognize that they have made a mistake. Instead, the goal should be for them to recognize their mistakes, learn from their mistakes, and then move on. You can also get them to recognize that they should not only learn from their mistakes but they should take action to remedy the problems that led to the mistakes. So, if they scored badly on an exam, that might mean spending the next hour studying. If they played poorly in a basketball game, it could mean spending more time practicing their jump shot. We don't want to get into a situation where high self-esteem means that we never admit failure. The purpose of having positive self-esteem is to recognize that our mistakes don't define us as a person. However, we also need to recognize that we should take action to improve our performance in the future.

One way that you can approach this with children is to help them convert their absolute statements into a remedy that turns the statement into a more positive outlook. So, you should not discourage them from recognizing their mistakes. Instead, you want to teach them to pair their mistakes with a solution to the mistake. So instead of saying "I never do good on math exams," you can have them say something to the effect of: "That exam didn't go as well as I hoped, but I am going to practice doing long division until I learn to do it right."

One question that is often raised when it comes to dealing with these situations with children is the following—people want to know if they have to be perfect in their outlook themselves, before they can help their children develop positive thought patterns. The answer to this question is: absolutely not. In fact, helping your children to develop more positive thought patterns is going to be an active exercise that will help you to develop more positive thought patterns yourself. So it can actually be a very healthy way for you to engage and help your own situation, while simultaneously helping your child to develop the power of positive thinking.

Chapter 3: The Levels of Self-Talk

As you develop and begin to combat the self-talk that has been holding you back in your life, there are going to be different levels of progress or actually different levels of your self-talk. In this chapter, we are going to go over the levels of self-talk that are generally accepted by psychologists.

Acceptance and Harmful Self-Talk

The type of self-talk at this level is uniformly negative. It's characterized by phrases such as "I am ..." followed by a negative statement. Common examples have already been discussed, but let's reproduce a few here:

I am ugly.

I am a total loser.

I am fat.

Statements that also indicate an inability to act also fall in this category. If you can't act to change something, that makes you a helpless victim, so these types of statements are common among people who have learned helplessness. The assertion that you are unable to act might be paired with an excuse of some kind. Examples could be:

I can't get into college because I'm stupid.

I can't earn enough money, because I didn't go to college.

I can't stick to any diet.

I can't lose weight; I have a thyroid problem.

Of course, having a thyroid problem and not having gone to college can be real problems that hold people back, but these are problems that can be rectified. The key point here is the *attitude* that underlies the statement. That attitude is one of defeatism and creates situations in our minds that cannot be overcome. Therefore, these are not only self-limiting statements, but they are also statements that justify the negative behaviors that are keeping us from moving forward.

Another common phrase that is used in harmful self-talk is: "If only …."

If only I was taller, girls would go out with me.

If only I was born rich, I could live in a nice neighborhood.

Self-talk statements that include the phrase "if only" are excuses for the situation you might be in. At the subconscious level, this works to reinforce limiting behaviors, and then the end results you experience are justified in your mind. Another form of this type of thinking is to use the statement "I wish …."

I wish I was smart, and then I could go to a good university.

I wish I was rich, and then I could get a new car.

Focus on the mentality that underlies the statements. The type of mentality expressed here is one that avoids taking action to change circumstances, and it also has an implied suggestion that your current situation is justified. For example, maybe you have an old beat-up car that is constantly breaking down. Rather than reacting by improving your credit score to get a loan or working more hours to get enough money to buy a new car, you justify the situation and put the desired goal in an unattainable spot.

When you engage in self-talk like this, the subconscious accepts these phrases as directions or programmed statements, and then it will generate destructive behaviors that act in a manner of self-fulfilling prophecy.

At the very beginning of this process, you are going to be at the level of "acceptance." So, in other words, this means that you actually believe and accept your negative self-talk. This is the level of self-talk that most of us are at when we seek help for the first time. So, all those negative statements that you're making to yourself, or—to be clear—that your subconscious is making about you, your conscious mind hears them and believes them to be true as well.

Recognizing Negative Self-Talk and the Need to Change It

If you are reading this book, then chances are you have already moved past the acceptance stage. That's because you have recognized that you have a negative self-talk problem. However, this doesn't mean that you have solved the situation.

Sometimes people that are in this stage are engaging in a lot of self-talk that expresses a desire for change but without actually taking any action on that change. So, in the acceptance stage—to use an example—you might be focused on telling yourself "I am fat." Whether or not that statement has some objective truth to it is not really our concern at the moment, we are simply noting that you are having the thought. If you have moved to the second level of self-talk, instead of simply having the thought "I am fat," you might have evolved into thinking, "I need to lose weight." Or you might have a thought such as: "I should start exercising." Another common phrase used at this stage is, "I need to do ...." Something to pay attention to here is that you can actually use this level of self-talk as a strategy for healing. If you are not experiencing this type of self-talk yet, and your self-talk remains mostly negative, try elevating things by moving to this type of self-talk on purpose, as a conscious exercise.

You can take this approach with all the levels of self-talk, in order to speed up the healing process. This works for many people, because it helps them to develop their abilities for positive thinking gradually and in stages, rather than trying to make a direct switch from negative to positive thinking. The types of statements at this level also help the conscious mind, because you are making a move from simply accepting the bad things in your life to recognizing that there is a need to make changes, and that more importantly, you are the agent of change.

For example, consider the following statement:

I can't lose weight. I am always going to be fat.

There are many ways that this statement can be turned into a statement that recognizes the need to make changes to improve the situation. Here is one way to do it:

I need to lose weight. I should start a diet that I am comfortable with.

This is a definite shift in thinking. Some people might proceed automatically through the levels of thought, but for most of us, making a conscious effort is going to be required.

In a definite sense, these types of thoughts are progress. Rather than simply being negative statements about our self-image, they have been changed into action statements. But, you will notice the phrases "I need ..." or "I should ...", and these are statements about the future without specific plans for taking action. And so, while we are making progress, this is far from an ideal situation.

One of the important steps to healing is not only recognizing that you are engaging in negative self-talk, but that you also take action to change it. So, when you are in a situation where you are saying to yourself: "I should do ..." or "I need to do ...", you are far from being healed when it comes to this problem. First of all, think of the phrase "I should ...." What are some of the things that this phrase conveys? I would say that one of the first things that comes to mind when I hear that phrase is that the person is not very serious about instituting change in their life. They have recognized that they have a problem, but they really haven't set a specific goal with a plan to reach that goal, in order to overcome the problem.

If you are in the stage where your thought processes are filled with a lot of "I should …" or "I need to …" type statements you need to write down each of these statements in a notebook. Then, for each statement of this type, develop a plan of action to start rectifying the problem. You want to break down your solution to each problem into three to five steps. So, this should be some type of practical approach that can actually be realized.

There are some types of negative self-talk that can be remedied by simply replacing them with positive thoughts. For example, "I'm ugly" is simply a statement. There isn't a practical approach that accompanies that statement. It's a relative statement that may or may not be based on reality at all. So, it's certainly one that is directly related to low self-esteem, and that should be replaced with a positive thought.

But if you find yourself engaging in any type of thought that could be characterized by the phrase "I should …" this is a thought that can be accompanied by action. That doesn't mean that we should automatically take action, however. You need to look at the thought process objectively and determine whether or not it really has validity. Sometimes, these types of thought processes are not valid. So, in those cases, you can simply throw them out by replacing them with positive thinking.

However, in some cases, those types of statements are going to be valid. Maybe you are ten pounds overweight. So, if you start saying to yourself "I should lose weight" rather than simply thinking "I am fat," it may be time to start taking action by writing down in your journal a plan to rectify the problem. Whatever plan you develop in your journal needs to have two steps. The first step is determining whether or not this is a real problem that is amenable to practical solutions. If not, you simply write down the positive statements to replace the negative thought. Then next time that you have negative thoughts, you replace them with a positive statement.

On the other hand, if this is something that you can act on, then write down the steps that you would take in order to rectify the problem. You should keep your steps in perspective. This means that you should set realistic goals that you can actually reach within a reasonable amount of time. Just to use one example to get a practical feel for this: suppose that you needed to lose 50 pounds. Losing 50 pounds is quite an achievement. So, as a matter of practicality, you probably aren't going to want to set losing 50 pounds as your goal. Instead, what you would do is set a goal of losing ten pounds and then come back to reevaluate the situation. For most goals, you can set down a three to five point plan and carry it out. I recommend putting specific dates in your plan, which will help to hold you accountable for actually carrying it out, and it will also help you get some perspective on the realistic possibilities that exist for solving the problem at hand.

Making a Decision to Change

The next level of self-talk is moving beyond phrases like "I should ..." and actually making a decision to change. This is a major elevation in character. When you are ready to move up to this level of self-talk, you are well on your way to healing and reprogramming your mind to get rid of the negative "software" that has been operating for so long and directing your results without you even realizing it.

One characteristic of this level is that you are fully rejecting the victim status that comes with learned helplessness. Rather than seeing yourself as floating through the world and being impacted solely by outside forces like "luck," you recognize that you are an agent for control and change in your life. At each level of self-talk, we are reprogramming the subconscious mind in stages. In fact, at the previous level, we've already recognized that we are not a victim, but this level takes things further by marrying that realization to the belief that we have the power to control our own lives. At each level, as you practice the new statements to replace the old ones, be sure to use a lot of repetition. As we discussed earlier, the subconscious mind learns through repetition and the more that you use this technique, the stronger that something is going to hold.

With that in mind, I don't recommend moving to higher levels of self-talk until you are seeing definite signs that you are making progress at the previous level. The signs you want to look for include a change in attitude. This should include, more importantly, a change in the self-talk that you are actually experiencing. Don't move forward until you truly feel that you are ready.

Think about tennis players. If a budding tennis player can barely hit the ball, should they keep practicing hitting the ball with a forehand swing, or should they start learning backhands and killer serves? I think that the answer to this question is they should become competent with the most basic forehand swing before moving on to learn more advanced methods. And what is happening in that case? We want the new tennis player to practice until the forehand swing enters the realm of the subconscious.

The same procedure is going to be used here. But when you are ready, you can start moving forward and improving your self-talk at this level. Let's go back and review what we did in the last level.

Writing a plan in your self-talk journal should indicate a duty to do something, but it does not indicate an actual decision to move forward and carry out the action. So, the next step in self-talk is to replace phrases by "I will …", "I will not …" and "never." These are phrases that indicate a definite course of action.

Try going through this by looking at the negative self-talk that you have written in your journal. Are there any negative thoughts that could be replaced by "I should …" and then "I will …" types of statements?

Here is an example. Suppose that a person finds it difficult to get to work or meet friends on time. The negative self-talk that may accompany this could be something to the effect of:

I'm always late.

Notice that this is a general and definite statement, as it includes the word "always." You should look for definite statements like this that can be replaced, to turn a general statement about you into a specific statement about a specific situation. Returning to the present exercise, the first step to move up to the second level of self-talk would be something like this:

I should get to work five minutes early.

This change has done two things. It first acknowledges the "duty" or obligation for the behavior by including the phrase "I should ..." in the self-talk. The second thing that this change has done is it has turned a general comment about the person into a specific criticism that is constructive, rather than acting as an attack on self-esteem or worth.

You can actually work on your negative self-talk in real-time by using this technique, once you've identified the thought that you want to change. This is going to require some conscious awareness in regard to the negative self-talk that appears in your head. The adjusted phrase will essentially be used as an affirmation. When you get the negative thought, consciously replace it with the new thought. You can also use the statement in regular affirmation sessions.

After you have done this for a few days, you need to turn this into a level 3 statement, which is going to be a direct statement of action, or of making a change. In this example, our new phrase is going to be the following:

I will arrive at work five minutes early each day.

Now we have a definite statement that is geared toward actually changing the problem behavior. You can use this as an affirmation and also say it when you recognize the negative self-talk appearing in your head.

This example was directed at a simple problem that can be changed with a direct statement. But readers may be wondering how to apply this to more general issues related to self-esteem, financial problems, relationship problems, or appearance. The fact is, this method can be applied in any situation. Typically, negative self-talk will result when a specific event happens. So, you might say to yourself, *"I'm a loser,"* but the statement probably doesn't occur in isolation. Look at the situation that triggered the thought. Then put the self-talk in context so that it can be reframed.

Let's use a simple example. Suppose a teenage boy approaches the girl of his dreams and she rejects him. A natural reaction to have inside his head is: "I'm such a loser." This could be turned around using the above method, by injecting some different contexts into the statement. Because one girl rejected the boy, that doesn't mean he is a "loser" in any general sense. The boy could move to the "I should …" phase by saying, "I should find another girl to ask out. She probably already had a boyfriend." This change creates an obligation that helps to reframe the situation and get rid of the general comment on self-worth. In fact, by replacing the reaction "I'm such a loser" with "I should find another girl to ask out, she probably already had a boyfriend," we have turned the focus outward and added an action that would remedy the immediate situation that led to the negative self-talk in the first place. This way, the self-talk is not going to work against self-esteem, and it's not general.

You can use this technique in almost any situation. Suppose that you need to lose some weight, and you've recently gone on a strict diet. But you're at a restaurant with some friends, and when the waiter comes around tempting you with desserts, you decide to get a piece of the pie. Afterward, you are going to be flooded with negative feelings for having made this mistake. As a result, you might be saying things to yourself like "I'm such a loser" or "I never do anything right." You might experience negative self-talk that makes reference to your weight or body image. These types of thoughts will be accompanied by definite statements. For example, this type of negative self-talk might include "I'll never lose weight" or "I'm always going to be fat." So, while these statements are not general attacks on self-esteem, at least on the surface, they include definite statements that indicate accomplishing the goal is impossible for you. In a sense, even though they don't seem general on the surface, they really are general comments on your abilities and will act to lower self-esteem.

Once again, we can put this type of negative self-talk into context and reframe the message. The goal is to focus on specific behaviors rather than making general comments on our self-worth. The first step in a situation like this is to acknowledge the mistake made. This is a little different from the last hypothetical situation we examined; in that case, there was not a mistake. But here there is a definite action we can point to. So, in this situation, you can acknowledge the mistake and then pledge to yourself to make changes in the future. You could replace any of the negative-self talk statements above with something like:

I made a mistake in ordering dessert. Next time I should politely decline.

The statement can be changed into a definite plan of action by turning the phrase "I should" into "I will."

Can-Do Self-Talk (Better You)

The previous level of self-talk turned negative self-talk into a definite statement related to changing behavior. Now we want to turn it into the type of self-talk that gives you power to change and take control over your life. This level of self-talk can include definite statements about your capability to take action and positive statements about your self-worth. For example, "I am …" is an important phrase in this level of self-talk, but rather than using it in a negative sense, you will use it in a positive statement.

I am smart and capable.

I am able to follow my diet and lose weight.

I am smart, interesting, and funny. I will get a date with the next girl.

I am in control of my financial life, and I am paying off my debts.

Any positive qualifier can be used at the can-do self-talk level. A common suggestion is to use the phrase: "Yes I can." This phrase includes a word that indicates definiteness, "Yes." It also includes a phrase with an assertion of your capacity to act: "I can."

Yes, I can stick to this diet and lose weight.

Yes, I can get to work five minutes early every day.

Universal Affirmation

The next level of self-talk elevates it to a spiritual level. This is the highest level of self-talk, and you should definitely move through all the previous levels before using universal self-talk. This level of self-talk can be used to express forgiveness, acceptance, and tolerance. This should begin with inward-directed thoughts. That is, you need to express forgiveness, acceptance, and tolerance toward yourself. Keep in mind that this is not an excuse for bad behaviors. Instead, it is a recognition that you are only human, and therefore you're going to be making mistakes. Forgiving yourself for making mistakes is a way to undo all the negative programming that has brought you to the point where you are now. Acceptance is a way to accept yourself for who you are. This is the opposite of saying, "I am such a loser." When you feel true acceptance, you realize that mistakes are going to be made in life but that these are not characteristic of you as a whole person, and they are not a reflection on your self-worth as a human being. Tolerance goes along with forgiveness. Again, this does not mean that you are endorsing the behaviors. This level of self-talk can be used in the form of affirmations that you say to yourself each day. Let's run through a couple of examples.

I am only human, and I forgive myself for making mistakes. I will do better next time.

I accept myself for who I am.

I accept myself and recognize I have flaws, but all human beings do.

You can also direct the universal affirmations outward.

Summary: The Five Levels of Self-Talk

Self-talk is an internal dialogue that tells us who we think we are. At this point, your internal self-talk is directed by years and even decades of negative programming that has been working in your subconscious mind, usually placed there or reinforced by external agents. These include your parents, caregivers, teachers, siblings, and peers. The five levels of self-talk explain different types of self-talk and give you a path forward that can be used to replace negative self-talk in a series of stages. This will turn the negative thinking into positive statements, and at first, it will take hard work and conscious effort. But like the tennis player who spends hours practicing, which turns their actions into automatic responses, the more you practice with the five levels of self-talk, the stronger and more automatic your positive self-talk is going to become. Remember that the subconscious mind is a blank slate, and I like to call it "dumb." That doesn't mean that the subconscious mind is not capable of producing large effects; if it couldn't, we wouldn't even be having this conversation. As we said earlier, by "dumb," I mean that the subconscious mind acts like a computer. It is ready to accept any programming that is given to it, and it will change accordingly. Of course, replacing old programming that has been ingrained for years is not easy, so have faith even if you don't get the results you want right away. Keep working at it until the old, negative programs are replaced by new can-do positive thinking.

Chapter 4: Stop the Blame Game

An unfortunate plague that can infect people with negative self-talk is the blame game. This can manifest in two different ways. The first way is in a constant effort by the person experiencing negative self-talk to blame other people and external factors for the circumstances they are in. So, you might blame your parents, or it's the fault of your boss that you have a lousy job. That would be in place of the rational view of the situation, which would be that if you have a job you don't like, find a new one instead of continuing to be in misery and focusing your energy on a lousy boss. We might recognize that having problems with your parents can influence your life, but it's something that you can overcome. This type of blame allows you to avoid taking responsibility for your situation.

Those whose lives are dominated by negative self-talk also blame themselves. In fact, some people fall squarely in this camp. Having low self-esteem is often accompanied by blaming yourself for everything that happens. One theme I have been emphasizing in this book is that you are an active agent capable of controlling your own future, but that doesn't mean that you have to blame yourself for each and every single situation. Self-blame is also not done in a constructive fashion. Instead, it is done in a way that reinforces negative thinking and serves to lower self-esteem even further. It will take the form of statements like: "I can't do anything right."

Blaming Someone Else for Your Problems

One of the reasons that people blame others for their circumstances is that they don't want to point the finger at themselves and lower their self-esteem even further. Remember that this all happens at the level of the subconscious, and the people who are experiencing this are not even aware that it's happening. It is human nature to want to protect your self-esteem and the image of yourself in your mind, even if you are plagued by negative thinking and already have low self-esteem. This can be called the fragile ego effect. It's also a result of dysfunctional thinking, in that the person with healthy thought processes would recognize that if they accept blame for a situation, that doesn't make them a bad person. Bad results from one incident or situation do not mean that you are a bad person overall or that you have no self-worth.

However, if you have dysfunctional thought processes related to self-esteem, you are prone to associate one mistake or bad action with the total destruction of your self-worth. So, in order to protect yourself from that kind of injury, you will project your blame outward.

Blaming someone else for our problems is a fairly common dysfunction. You can randomly approach people on the street, and it won't take long before you find someone who can blame others for their circumstances. We already gave a common example. How hard is it to find a person who will blame their boss for a poor work environment? If you dig deeper, you are likely to find that this person blames others for different circumstances in their life.

For this kind of person, everything bad that happens is somebody else's fault. It also protects them from the need to make changes to the way they think and live. So, the guy who says his lousy work-life is the fault of his boss also blames the banks or credit card companies for his massive debt that makes it hard for him to pay the bills each month. It's always going to be someone else that is the root cause of all his problems. If he is married, then it's going to be his wife's fault. The blame game is a convenient defense mechanism because you can always find an external agent on which to cast blame. The blame game can be said to be a mentality where "anyone but me" is at fault. This is an interesting expression of negative self-talk, that while rooted in low self-esteem, it expresses itself through projection, casting blame on others who might have some influence in your life, whether they are at fault or not. Usually, in interpersonal relations, unless it's a situation that involves outright abuse, both people are contributing. Why not look at your own contributions to bad situations instead of casting the blame on others?

Are you partaking in the blame game?

Start looking at the bad situations in your life. Write them down on a sheet of paper. Maybe you have too much debt that you aren't able to pay off. Maybe you hate your job. Write all of these situations down—but don't write down the rational explanation for them. Write down the thoughts you've been telling yourself about them. Note when you are blaming someone else.

The first step in a "blaming others" situation is to take a step back and try to look at the situation objectively. This is not an easy thing to do. But the key here is to look at the role you are playing in the situation.

If you hate your job and blame your boss, who is difficult to get along with, there are several questions you can ask yourself. Is the problem really your boss? What role are you playing in your relationship with the boss? Maybe you show up to work late, or maybe you work at a slow and unproductive pace. Maybe when the boss criticizes you, you tend to take it personally (very common among those who are suffering from negative self-talk). Try and think of the roles that you are actually playing in the situation and in your relationships that could be contributing to the problem.

If you are able to identify some ways that you are contributing to the problem, then take it to the next step. Write down the opposite behaviors that would end your contribution to the problem. It might be as simple as changing the tone of voice you use when your boss criticizes you for something. Instead of reacting negatively, thank her for pointing out the things you were doing wrong, and promise to work harder to improve your performance. If you are showing up to work late, start showing up to work early. Try to find at least three situations that are within your power to change.

The next step is to implement the new behaviors for a month. Think about it; a month is not really a long time at all. See how it goes for a month, and then re-evaluate your relationship with your boss and your feelings about the job after making the changes. Even if you don't see an improvement, this is a good exercise in avoiding casting blame, and instead focusing on taking action to implement changes. However, chances are you are going to see improvement in the dynamics of the interaction along with a better overall feeling about the job and the relationship you are having with your boss.

If your job is objectively lousy, ask yourself what you are doing about it. Are you even looking for a new job? Or are you simply running in place, and then continually complaining about it?

When it comes to interpersonal interactions, blaming those who are closest to us for our problems is quite a common occurrence. How many people have blamed their parents for where they are in their lives now? Let's be clear—your parents can have a very big influence, and if it was not positive, then the negative programming that they plugged into your subconscious mind can be causing problems. But are they at fault, decades later? If you are an adult, it's time for you to take responsibility for the position that you are in with your life at this very moment. That doesn't mean completely forgetting the negative programming that was put into your subconscious by others when you were a child, but you need to take responsibility for reprogramming your subconscious and avoid casting blame on others. You are not a victim.

Another common method of deflection that is used is called labeling. In fact, we've been seeing self-directed labeling throughout the book. Labeling takes the form of attaching some general, self-defeating characteristic to yourself. A common example is to say: "I am stupid." But labeling can also play a role in the blame game when you deflect blame onto others. In a work situation or interpersonal relationship, when casting blame on the people around us, we also label them, for example: "My wife is stubborn." If you see that you are using labeling to put other people in boxes, you should adjust your thinking, in the same way that you would adjust your thinking for your own negative self-talk. In fact, this is just another example of self-talk, even though it's directed toward others, and its purpose is to absolve yourself from taking responsibility.

Try looking for actions you are taking that could lead to the apparent validity of the attribute that you have given as a label to someone. So maybe we can turn "My wife is stubborn" into:

My wife won't talk when I yell.

This statement recognizes that there is behavior exhibited by the wife that could be interpreted as her being stubborn, but it has also recognized the role that you are playing in the situation. We can use this in other situations as well.

My boss is a jerk.

After determining actions that you are taking to cause your boss to behave in an abrasive manner, you might say this instead:

My boss is short-tempered when I show up to work late.

This identifies your own behavior that may have contributed to the situation. Of course, this does not completely absolve your boss. If you start showing up to work early and your boss continues to be short-tempered, then maybe your boss does have issues. But in that case, it is still your responsibility to fix the situation—in this case, by finding a new job that is a better fit for you.

Sometimes casting blame takes the form of abstractions. So, there isn't really a specific person to blame. Maybe you are not making enough money to make ends meet. Instead of taking action by looking for a second job or working more hours, or working toward getting a promotion and higher pay, you blame the external circumstances. You'll blame the job itself, or blame the company, rather than looking for ways to improve your own situation.

Casting blame on others for your circumstances is no minor issue. It's a major flaw in your thought processes, and it's going to be holding you back in your life. If you are finding that you are often blaming others for your circumstances or bad things that happen in your life, it's time to change this way of thinking. Start by writing down any occasion when you catch yourself blaming others or attributing blame in an abstract sense. Then write down the role that you are playing in each situation. Once you have figured that out, write down the steps you can take to change your role in the situation. This is not a guarantee that the situation will change, but certainly, in most cases, it will improve. But remember you can't just write down the steps for change—you are going to need to actually carry them out.

Blaming Yourself

The other extreme is blaming yourself for everything. The last section does illuminate the fact that when there are conflicts and bad situations, we often play a role in the circumstances. However, it's also true that we are not to blame for every single thing that happens. Self-blame can be as destructive as blaming others. There is a fine line between taking responsibility for making mistakes and blaming yourself for everything that happens. If you are facing negative self-talk and the destructive thought processes and attitudes that go along with it, this can mean that blaming yourself for everything is part of the dysfunctional pattern and will only lead to lower self-esteem.

Blaming yourself takes a familiar form. Self-blame will include statements like "I should have done ..." or "If only I had done ...

then ...." You will constantly be telling yourself: "It's my fault this happened."

Again, there is a fine line, because it's important to recognize that in many cases, bad things that happen are our own fault. But besides recognizing that we contribute to situations and that many people or circumstances might be responsible, the way that we react to situations that we are at fault for is as important as the recognition itself.

The unhealthy way to respond to this kind of situation is to see that you are at fault, blame yourself, and then wallow in depression about it. This is usually accompanied by a general crash in self-esteem. The healthy way to respond to a situation that you played a role in creating is to acknowledge the mistakes you made, and then make a plan to learn from the mistakes and do better next time. You should acknowledge the mistakes you make without blaming yourself and without blowing the mistakes out of proportion, so that they don't turn into an overall evaluation of your worth as a human being.

If you feel that you are at fault for a bad outcome or event that has happened, and other people are involved, try offering an apology for your actions. Don't make a big deal about it but apologize. If possible, include an action that will help to rectify the situation with your apology. This will help mend your relationships with other people and can prompt expressions of forgiveness. It will also promote tolerance and acceptance among those who are around you. They are going to appreciate the fact that when you have made a mistake, you are willing to take responsibility for it. The positive energy that this will create will help to elevate your good and positive feelings, and that, in turn, will help to direct your self-talk in a more positive direction.

When you are suffering from the first level of negative self-talk, your subconscious is directing your mood and actions through negative programming. One side effect of this is that negative events are not time-limited in your mind. This is a result of the fact that you tend to blow things out of proportion. It's also a result of generalizing. So, if you made a mistake at work that caused a lot of problems, you'll generalize it to impact your overall feelings of self-esteem and self-worth. These feelings are, in a sense, permanent and timeless without intervention. Therefore, you will remove the time-limited aspect that should be associated with the problem, and you might even make it permanent. Relatively minor bad events are normally localized in nature, and healthy people move on from them in a short time. But if your mindset is dominated by negative programming, you might find this difficult or impossible.

Affirmations can help here. Use affirmations that acknowledge that you made a mistake, but that you will do better next time and you're moving on. Also, redirect your mind. As each day passes, new situations and issues arise. If you find your mind wandering back to the troublesome event, remind yourself that it was in the past and doesn't matter anymore, and replace the thoughts about it by current concerns, no matter how minor they are.

Manipulative Blame

Another unhealthy way to use the blame game is to do so in a manipulative fashion. If you are engaging in this type of behavior, it is probably happening on an unconscious level, so you should forgive yourself for doing so. But it is important to recognize this behavior and end it, because blaming either yourself or others in a manipulative way is a toxic behavior.

In rare cases, people who are narcissistic or sociopathic will use blame in a conscious manner in order to manipulate people. However, we are going to ignore that for the purposes of this discussion. If you find someone in your life that is engaging in that kind of behavior, that is someone that you definitely want to avoid.

One way that manipulative blame is used is to generate sympathy. So, in this case, it's going to be self-blame. Again, we are ignoring the case of a sociopath that consciously uses this as a "technique" to manipulate others, that kind of topic is beyond the scope of this book. What we are talking about here are otherwise normal people who are suffering from low self-esteem and negative thought processes. In this case, you aren't really conscious of doing it, but you will blame yourself in order to draw the sympathy of others, in a misguided attempt to get others to pay attention to you and reinforce your self-esteem.

This is a hard one to accept and move past, but if you find yourself engaging in this type of behavior, forgive yourself. Adopt an attitude of tolerance and acceptance and pledge to avoid doing it in the future. Becoming aware of the behavior is the first step that you can take in your journey to interacting with others in a healthier fashion. When you are in a situation where you are feeling the urge to accept blame, and you can recognize when it might be a case of actually directing sympathy toward yourself, consciously recognize the self-talk that is going on at the time leading you toward taking this kind of action. Use that to replace it with thoughts that are more positive and uplifting.

Another case of manipulative blame is immediately casting blame on others, to avoid taking the responsibility yourself. Of course, we have discussed this situation in the context of self-talk, but in this situation, we are considering the person who does this publicly so that blame is actually shifted. Again, the first step is recognition of the problem. If you are doing this, become consciously aware of the situation and the negative thought processes that can cause you to take negative actions that impact others. Replace these thoughts by more positive thoughts, and also thoughts that increase your own self-responsibility.

Chapter 5: Confronting Negative Self Talk

In this chapter, we are going to focus more closely on the process of confronting negative self-talk for the purpose of eliminating it. This is an important step in the process of healing yourself from years of negative programming. The first step in confronting negative self-talk is to recognize it when it happens in real-time. This can actually be a very difficult process. Think about all the years that have gone by and you've been experiencing negative self-talk, and all of this is going on at a subconscious level. That means the most basic step of all, which is simply recognizing negative self-talk when it occurs, can be very difficult for some people. But if you are willing to put the required work in to do this, you will make progress on this issue very quickly.

Once you have recognized negative self-talk, you need to know what to do with it. The purpose here is to label it and replace it with positive self-talk.

Recognizing Negative Self-Talk

It's one thing to talk about negative self-talk in a book, or even to write down some negative self-talk that you've experienced, in a journal. It can be quite another thing to actually recognize it in real-time. Since this is so difficult, it's going to take some work. The fact is you have gone your entire life experiencing negative thoughts flowing through your mind without actually being aware that it's happening. So, it's hard to focus when these thoughts are just unconsciously flowing through your mind—often when you're busy with other things. The easiest way to recognize negative self-talk is when it happens in a specific situation. For example, somebody may upset you, or maybe you made a mistake of some kind.

That is hard enough as it is to do in real-time. It's even worse when you're not directly involved in a bad situation, but you're having negative thoughts that are often quite subtle in nature, flowing through your head throughout the day. You might be having negative thoughts while driving to work, or when you're sitting at your desk going through emails. Or you might have negative thoughts if you're doing something as simple as browsing Facebook. So, in these situations, your mind is focused on the task at hand, and the negative thoughts are occurring in the background. In that case, it may be hard to recognize them. Of course, when you are in the midst of a bad experience, it will be easier to recognize the negative thoughts that are occurring in relation to that experience.

The first step that you can take is to have awareness. Part of that awareness is to familiarize yourself with the kinds of words and phrases that commonly appear in negative self-talk. It's impossible to present an exhaustive list, but you can write down your own list and see what you come up with. Some of the words that could be included are: stupid, dumb, inept, failure, wrong, if only, I wish, I always, I can't, perfect, what's the point, there is no use, I'm not worthy, I'm a loser, I'm not worth it, I'll never change, I can't change, and things will never change.

Try sitting down and seeing if you can expand this list, using your own negative thoughts as a guide.

Catching Yourself Using Negative Self-Talk

The first step that you need to use in this process is catching yourself in the act. You're going to have to put in some effort, and I am talking about conscious effort, to catch yourself engaging in the negative self-talk. So, each morning when you get up you should meditate on this for a few minutes. Commit yourself to recognizing negative self-talk when it occurs throughout the day. As I said in the last section, this is not going to be easy, so you can forgive yourself ahead of time for missing a lot of the negative self-talk that happens on autopilot.

However, after you start committing to doing this, you are going to find that it will become easier to spot negative thoughts as they occur. This is going to require a heightened sense of self-awareness. I have to say that there are going to be multiple benefits that you will experience in engaging in this exercise.

Begin by simply recognizing when the negative thought occurs. Then, make a conscious effort to make a statement reflecting the negative thoughts back. So, let's just say that a negative thought is: "I am a loser." When you notice yourself saying this, pause for a minute and then say to yourself (in your mind if necessary), "I just had the thought that I am a loser."

Although we are anxious to see improvement in our lives, when we take things a little bit slowly, we do a more thorough job in healing, and we will see better results down the road. Therefore, you should practice simply recognizing the negative thoughts and self-talk that you're having throughout the day, and pause to notice them on a conscious level. Do this for about a week. You will find that as time goes on and you practice this skill more, you will catch more and more negative thoughts as they flow through your head. This will help you to defeat them and replace them with positive thoughts later on.

Negative thought patterns and self-talk can often cause a higher level of stress on the body. If you notice that you are feeling tense, achy, or tired when having a lot of negative thoughts, then as you recognize them do some deep breathing exercises. Begin to increase your awareness that the supposed "truths" contained in the negative self-talk are not truths at all, but are usually in fact exaggerations if not outright false statements. This kind of recognition will help to bring down the stress level that negative self-talk creates. It will lessen the impact of the negative self-talk, both mentally and physically.

Labeling Negative Self-Talk

You should use multiple types of labeling when addressing negative thoughts. In addition to labeling your negative self-talk as "just a thought," you can label the statement as "false." For example, consider the following negative statement:

I can't speak up during the meeting, because I will sound stupid.

Let's label this statement as nothing more than a thought, and then make sure that we emphasize that it's not true. So, we could say:

I just had the thought that if I speak up in the meeting, I will sound stupid. It's not true.

Now we have taken the process of recognizing our negative self-talk two steps further. By labeling the self-talk as a "thought," we work to diminish its importance. Second, we have recognized that it is not a true statement.

Telling Your Negative Thoughts to F-Off

We can carry this exercise a step further. After you have labeled the negative thought, you can tell it to go away. How you go about doing this is up to you, but basically, you want to tell the thought to disappear from your mind. You can do this with a simple wave of the hand in the beginning.

Spend a few days attacking your negative thoughts in this manner. Simply getting rid of them and minimizing their importance is a major step forward. The more time that your mind spends without negative thoughts, the better off you will be. In fact, this is a positive in and of itself, even though you might not have replaced it with a positive thought.

As part of the process of getting rid of negative self-talk, you can carefully examine the statements that are causing you the most trouble. Remember that people who are suffering from negative self-talk and the types of programming that give rise to it, are often the kinds of people who make mountains out of molehills. In other words, they blow things out of proportion and overreact. Take a look at the situations that give rise to your own negative self-talk and see if you aren't engaging in this type of behavior yourself. Also, I recall our discussion about the time-limiting nature of most mistakes and problems. Each time that you find yourself having a negative thought, ask yourself if this is a problem that is going to be causing problems over the long-term.

Second, don't make assumptions. One problematic response that people engage in, which leads to negative thoughts, is making assumptions about the intentions of others. When your subconscious mind is governed by negative programming, this usually takes the form of assuming that other people are thinking negative thoughts about you. In fact, these can be specific instances of negative self-talk. "I know she thinks I am stupid," or "My manager thinks I am worthless." Try catching yourself in these kinds of negative thought patterns as well. While you are not directly labeling yourself, in reality, you are still engaging in labeling, but you are projecting the labeling onto others. So instead of calling yourself stupid, you are asserting to yourself that someone else thinks you are stupid when you would usually have no objective evidence that this is really the case.

Of course, this reminds us that we should eliminate generalized labels from our self-talk. So, you want to eliminate things like "I am completely hopeless" or "I am stupid" from your self-talk.

Also, avoid the all-or-nothing fallacy that comes along with black-and-white thinking. There are very few situations that fall into this category, so you want to get that type of thinking out of your mind in most circumstances. Don't view a single event in your life as either all good or all bad, and don't inflate the importance of any one event. Most events are very time-limited and don't have that big of an impact. Have some awareness of when this is the case.

Changing Perspectives

This is difficult to do, but when you are troubled by a situation or event, try putting yourself in someone else's shoes. It might not be easy to see yourself from other perspectives, so instead, you might want to try imagining how your behavior would look if someone else did it. Maybe you were at work, and you made a remark in a meeting that everyone seemed to ignore. So, you tell yourself how stupid you are, and that you should just avoid speaking up in meetings so that you won't reinforce the perception that you are dumb. Catch yourself in these thoughts and label them and tell them to go away. Then imagine one of your coworkers speaking up as you did. When you do this, it will help you to realize how minor the event really was, and you will recognize that you would not have thought that the person was "stupid" for having spoken up. This will make it a little bit easier to see that you also aren't looking that way to others. Try using a change of perspective whenever the interaction involves multiple people. This is also going to help you see the time-limited nature that characterizes many interactions that we blow out of proportion in our own minds.

Changing perspective can also help you communicate more effectively and in a healthier manner in general, by the way. For those times that you did actually make a mistake in your communication, it helps if you can try seeing it from someone else's perspective.

Replacing Negative Thoughts

The final step in this process is to start training your mind to have positive thoughts instead. This process can be a bit nuanced. Remember that in the last chapter we discussed how easy it is to blame other people for our own situations, and so sometimes we have to replace our negative thoughts while recognizing the role that we play in creating our own reality. In this case, it is not going to be some feel-good session of just talking yourself up. You should work to replace the negative thoughts you are having with positive thoughts that are realistic in what they say.

To get started, we need to consider how a healthy person engages in positive thinking. Simply wishing upon a star is not something that can be called "healthy." So, you should not engage in artificial self-esteem building, and you don't want to set up pie in the sky expectations that are impossible to realize. You should also avoid vague generalizations.

Keep in mind that generalized positive thoughts like "I'm good enough" or "I am smart and confident" are good to include in your affirmations. In this case, we are talking about replacing specific negative thoughts that are occurring in your daily life, often about specific issues and situations.

Positive self-talk should affirm your value without being egocentric. It should be supportive while recognizing the mistakes you make and the role that you play in different situations. Positive self-talk will often invoke a specific plan that can actually be accomplished. It will recognize the mistakes that occur and rather than using them to punish yourself and emphasize your own lack of self-worth, positive self-talk will focus on generating a plan of action to correct the mistakes and move forward.

Let's look at some negative and positive self-talk examples for a few situations, to see ways that you can turn around negative self-talk and replace it with a positive statement. A positive statement, as we said above, isn't necessarily going to be a completely win-win statement or something that puts your head in the clouds, it will be a realistic statement that can recognize problems without completely destroying your own self-esteem and self-worth.

Here is an example of a negative statement:

I am so stupid! I should just keep my mouth shut in meetings. Nobody even heard what I said. I looked like a total weirdo.

This could be replaced by a more realistic statement, such as:

I know I can do better. I am going to practice speaking louder and more clearly so that people will be able to hear what I have to say. I have interesting and insightful things to share in our meetings.

Another example of a negative thought:

I am not going to bother dieting anymore! I cheat every time. I am never going to lose weight!

This can be replaced by a more realistic positive statement:

I made a mistake in eating dessert. Next time I am going to refuse it, and I am going to devote more time to exercise.

The difference between a negative self-talk statement and a positive self-talk statement isn't so much that we are simply feeling good about ourselves, but instead, we are removing personal attacks that we make on ourselves and our own self-worth. These are replaced by facts about the situation, possibly including the recognition that we made a mistake, and then a plan of action to do better in the future.

Negative self-talk avoids any suggestion that there is a way to solve the problems at hand. It simply focuses on destroying whatever self-esteem you have left, and turns a generalization from a single error into a feeling of complete unworthiness. When you engage in negative self-talk, the interpretation of the situation is completely unrealistic, blown out of proportion, and made completely general.

Consider a professional basketball player—let us suppose that they are married and have children at home. One day the player has a bad game, and continually makes mistakes in the game. Positive self-talk after the game would recognize the problems that were specific to that one situation. So, the player might say, "I should practice more, and make sure I get a good night's sleep before the game." This type of self-talk is realistic and offers a prescription that is specific to that situation—performing badly in one single game. If the player had negative self-talk, they might say to themselves "I'm such a loser! I should just quit the team! My children probably don't want even to see me, so maybe I won't even go home!"

That kind of generalization is completely unrealistic. Although this might be seen as an extreme example, when you look at your own self-talk, you'll see that the highlighted reaction is also not really an exaggeration. You might be engaging in that kind of self-talk on a daily basis yourself. It's easy to see how ridiculous it is when we imagine someone else engaging in negative self-talk—particularly when they are in a high position of achievement like "professional basketball player." But this helps to illustrate how imagining others having the same thoughts and feelings can help you put your self-talk in perspective.

Getting Rid of Negative Self-Talk and Replacing it Can Change How You Feel

The first few times you recognize your negative self-talk and then eliminate it, think about how this makes you feel. You are probably going to find that this relieves the amount of stress that you are feeling in your life and that it's also going to improve your self-esteem. In a small way, it is taking control of your own life. And actually, it's quite a big improvement, because taking control over your self-talk is a way to change the entire direction of your life. You can then see how changing your self-talk by replacing negative thoughts with positive statements changes the way that you feel. Pay attention to not only how it makes you feel, but also see if you start noticing the direction of your life changing. At first, you might start to see that your behavior is changing as a result of the new programming that you are instilling in your mind. As a result of your new behaviors, you are probably also going to see better life results.

Chapter 6: Fostering Self Esteem

A large part of overcoming the negative programming that has been a part of your life for so many years, involves fostering your own self-esteem. You want to reach a point where your self-esteem is positive and healthy without being narcissistic. That means you need to recognize your own value and contributions while having a realistic interpretation of them. One of the problems has been the negative programming that you've been experiencing; it essentially makes you your own bully.

People who have negative programming and engage in negative self-talk are constantly putting themselves down. You don't need anyone else to do it for you—you are your own worst enemy. So, you need to start there by ending the self-criticism that constantly puts you down. From here, you can start fostering self-worth and self-esteem and then become, what I like to call, "a leader of self."

Stop Being Your Own Bully

The worst thing about negative programming in the self-talk that it generates is that we are constantly putting ourselves down. The criticism that we offer ourselves is general in nature, and so we reject our own self-value and our own uniqueness. This is a theme that has been running through the book, but it bears repeating. The problem with negative self-talk—among other things—is that the criticism that it engenders actually puts you down as a person, rather than focusing on specific mistakes or errors that you have made. I'm sure that you recognize in other people the fact that they can still have value even when they make a mistake. The problem is that you are not holding yourself to your own standards.

Recognizing Yourself as Worthy

The first step in healing, so that you can foster self-esteem, is recognizing that you have your own self-worth. You are a unique human being that is as special as anyone else. It's true that you have your own flaws, but we all do. You also have your own strengths and skills that have been combined in a completely unique way, which makes you a special individual.

Try developing some affirmations that focus on the strengths that you know you have. You can say these to yourself a couple of times a day to recognize your own worthiness as a human being. You can also try to keep them in mind to use, in order to replace negative thoughts that you have about your own self-worth during the day.

Steps to Foster Self-Love and Self-Esteem

Often times, negative thought processes and self-talk arise when you have had a negative experience of some type. Maybe you made a mistake, or you perceive that you made a mistake. Or maybe you've had a conflict with somebody. Many times, when we get in arguments, if we have low levels of self-love and self-esteem, we will be prone to blaming ourselves and feeling negative.

One important way to deal with these situations is to focus on the issue at hand, and the specific behaviors themselves, without focusing on yourself as a person. That way, you can reject the mistake or the behavior that you may have engaged in, while still recognizing your value as a person. This will help to keep your self-esteem intact, even when you've made bad decisions or behaved in a bad manner.

Something else that you need to do is not bring up things that happened in the past in the context of current situations. Often times, as we've noted, people who are suffering from negative programming have a tendency to dwell on the past. Once again, I'm not saying to forget the past, but don't use current difficulties as an excuse to bring up the past and punish yourself for doing it again.

Another problem that we all have—to one extent or another—is comparing ourselves to other people. This is a mental exercise that you should avoid engaging in. Comparing yourself to others unless you are looking to them for inspiration is not helpful. You don't want to be comparing yourself to other people if you are going to end up putting yourself down in the process. This only serves to tear down whatever self-esteem that you may have. So, something to avoid is looking at another person and saying: "Well, they always get it right, and I always get it wrong." That is not a helpful way to compare yourself to another person.

And in fact, if you are looking to other people for inspiration, you shouldn't do it in the manner of comparing yourself to them. Instead, you should use them as an example of how you could change the way you act in certain situations, or maybe you're inspired by the level of education or training somebody has obtained. In that case, you might say to yourself: "Well, I can do what they do when they are in a difficult situation," or alternatively "I'm going to get the kind of education that they got." You should reframe any examples that involve other people and where they are positioned in their life, rather than simply comparing yourself to them in order to put yourself down.

Another thing to consider in these types of situations is the fact that your negative outlook on life reflects itself as a negative thought process. You should start looking at the positives instead. Let's refer back to the chapter where I discussed a set of dysfunctional ways to look at situations that I called "the reality distortion field." If you recall, one of the dysfunctional ways of interpreting situations that psychologists have identified is called filtering. To refresh your memory, what happens is that people who engage in filtering tend to focus on the negative aspects of a situation. And so, what happens in these people is they ignore the positives that are sure to be there in any experience.

Are you doing this in your own life?

Try filtering the other direction. I don't want to emphasize this too much because I don't want to get into a "goody-feely" type of outlook. So, in other words, I'm not going to advise that you do filtering and only focus on the positive aspects of an interaction or situation. There may be negative things happening that you need to be aware of in order to learn from your mistakes. But what I am saying is that you should keep your eye out for the positives as well as the negatives and give yourself credit where credit is due. This is especially true when you are working on changing yourself and improving your situation. That's because when we are learning, we are still going to be more prone to seeing negative aspects of the situation and even toward making more mistakes than usual. One of the reasons that we make more mistakes is that if we are constantly blaming others or engaging with negative thoughts, there is no reason to improve ourselves. So, don't be discouraged if it's harder to find positive aspects of the situation. Be happy when you find them and praise yourself for them.

Let's take a couple of practical examples. Earlier in the book, we used the example of speaking out in a meeting, and maybe that's not something you normally do. So perhaps you were nervous and didn't speak loud enough for people to hear you clearly, and so they might not have said anything in response, and it appeared that they were ignoring you or not valuing what you had to say. When discussing this situation earlier, I mentioned that you could replace your interpretation of the event with a pledge to do better next time. But there are also positives in this experience. If you have previously been nervous about speaking up in meetings, even if the particular event did not go well, you should congratulate yourself for having the courage to speak out. You should also remind yourself that your opinions and your contributions matter.

Another important step in fostering your self-esteem is recognizing that things don't always progress in a linear fashion. So, you are not going to get rid of your negative self-talk all in one go. You are also not going to feel better about all your situations or change your bad behaviors in a perfectly consistent manner that progresses from day to day. It's going to be important to recognize that sometimes you're going to take a step forward, while other times you might find yourself taking two steps back. But at other times, you are going to take three steps forward and make serious progress.

And the truth is that even when you have setbacks, you are still making progress. Once you get going on this, remember that it wasn't that long ago when you were completely trapped by your negative thought processes. When things don't seem to be going the right way, don't worry about it and just keep on doing the exercises.

You can also always refer to your self-talk journal. Don't just keep a journal for the sake of recording negative thoughts. Also, record the positive thoughts and changes in behavior that you are seeing. That way, you can use the journal to help yourself get a more realistic view of how things are progressing. Imagine that at the start of a new week you have several days in a row of bad experiences and negative thoughts that you can't seem to get out of. In a situation like that, you might consider going back to the journal and reviewing your past progress. This will help boost your mood and self-esteem, and help you realize that progress is going to involve some occasional setbacks. This way, you can avoid getting all down and depressed about it.

Take Up Hobbies or Volunteer

One of the things that often contributes to negative thought processes is a mild level of depression. So many people who are suffering from negative self-talk are slightly depressed. But they are not really depressed enough to possibly even notice it or even get treatment for it. For that kind of low-level depression, going on medication is certainly not recommended in any situation. Instead, you should look to change your external life, to help foster good feelings and purpose in life.

One way that you can do this is by taking up some hobbies or volunteering. Many people will read this and start grumbling that they don't have time. Try not to make excuses—and find the time when you can do something. If you aren't sure about what you might be interested in, get out a piece of paper and write down different activities or sports, or passions that could be used for volunteering. Then figure out how to get involved in doing these, maybe just once or twice a week.

This will have a great impact on your life. For one thing, it will help you to make more connections with other people in situations that are not really judgmental. For example, if you take up a hobby that is innocuous, like bird watching, this is something that you can just do for fun and to meet other people without worrying about acquiring some massive skill set and impressing people. I also encourage people to take up activities that get them outdoors.

Two of the side benefits of this include elevating your mood. Simply engaging with other people in a shared activity that doesn't involve work or family responsibilities is going to go a long way toward elevating your mood. Second, if you can get one or more hobbies that involve being outdoors, this alone is going to help elevate your mood. You are also going to find your mind distracted a bit by your interest in the hobby.

The end result of this is that you are going to find yourself feeling better about yourself. Your mind is going to have less time to engage in negative thinking, and the elevation of your mood is actually going to change the state of your brain so that you will naturally drift toward higher levels of self-love and self-esteem.

Perhaps the ideal situation would be to take up one hobby and one volunteering interest. By volunteering, you can help take some of the focus off yourself and turn it toward a cause that is greater than self. It really doesn't matter what you pick, but it should have some kind of higher purpose. Volunteering will help you connect with like-minded folks, and the shared passion about the cause will help to alleviate negative thinking patterns. It's also going to help elevate your self-esteem, in part because you are getting some new purpose in your life, while also getting involved in something that has a larger purpose beyond just individual matters. One of the problems that we have in our society today is that there is an excessive focus on activities that are only designed to entertain us individually. So, we are spending too much time watching Netflix, listening to music, trying to develop the perfect body, or playing video games. In my view, it can go a long way if you spend a little bit of time focused outward instead of inward.

Building a Foundation of Self-Esteem

In order to build a foundation of self-esteem, you should start by adopting an attitude of unconditional love. This might sound a little bit strange, but you're going to need to apply that unconditional love to yourself. If you don't love yourself and accept yourself the way you are, nobody else is going to be able to love or respect you either.

Unconditional love means that you love yourself the way you are and accept the fact that you are not perfect. When you make mistakes, you need to recognize them within this type of context.

Tolerance and acceptance are part of unconditional love. You should also forgive yourself for wrongdoing. Again, this does not mean that you allow yourself to get by continually making wrong decisions or making mistakes without learning from them. What we are after here is not conflating bad behavior with the person. As part of this exercise, you might learn to do that with other people.

In some cases, people that are really hard on themselves are also hard and extra judgmental when it comes to their opinions about other people. So, you can also work on building a foundation for your own self-esteem by applying these principles to other people. You might even do it to the people that you have the most difficulties in your life with, such as your boss at work. Be forgiving and understand that sometimes people interact in unhealthy ways because of problems they are having at home. Your boss could have a serious illness that you don't know about, or maybe she just had an argument with her husband before coming to work. A coworker may be having financial problems that make them a little bit grouchy.

And of course, other people besides yourself simply make mistakes. So, try adopting an attitude of forgiveness, tolerance, and acceptance, and apply it to yourself and also to those around you.

Another way to foster self-esteem is to drop the expectations you have from others. That doesn't mean that you become a rug and let people walk all over you. You should definitely demand respect and decent treatment from other people. But stop expecting other people to acknowledge your achievements or contributions. Be happy when they do but ignore it when they don't. A lot of times, we set ourselves up for negative self-talk and thought processes if we expect too much out of other people. One of the most important things that I learned is that other people don't always have you as the focus in their life. They have a lot of other things on their mind, and so you might be number ten on their list. This is not a reflection on your inherent value or importance. So, don't take it that way, but just realize all the mistakes and errors that you make in your interactions with others are not necessarily as important to them as they are to you. This is going to help foster self-esteem because then you will realize that sometimes when other people aren't reacting to you, it has nothing to do with you at all, and there's no reason to engage in negative thought processes as a result.

Becoming a Leader of Self

Realizing that you have the power to control your own life is one of the most important steps to eliminating negative self-talk and thoughts from your mind. It's important to recognize that when you have the power to control your own life, while it's not complete power, you do have some control over the outcomes that you experience. This is a very different attitude than attributing everything to luck or connections. It's also very empowering. However, it comes with a certain level of taking responsibility.

If you have the power to control your own life and its outcomes, that means you need to take responsibility when things are not going the way that you want them to. This can be hard for some people to accept. Especially if you were going through your life blaming other people for the situation and circumstances that you are in now. In fact, the concept of blame has no place when you take responsibility for yourself.

Taking responsibility means that you are going to take the correct actions that are necessary in order to get good outcomes. Keep in mind that no outcome is guaranteed. However, you are still going to need to take the right steps to make progress in your life. When you're doing this, the outcomes will depend a lot more on you, as opposed to sitting around having negative thoughts that prevent you from taking action.

Taking responsibility also means righting the ship when you have made mistakes that hurt others. So be prepared to admit your mistakes to yourself and to others, and then to take action to rectify the problems that may have happened as a result of your past behaviors.

One thing that you will find when you take control over your life in this way is that the negative thought processes that you've had for so long simply vanish. Instead, you are going to be thinking in a more realistic and positive fashion that is going to involve making progress instead of wallowing the way that you have been with negative self-talk.

Chapter 7: Emotional Intelligence

Managing the self-talk that governs your life also involves managing your emotions. In turn, you are going to have to manage how you react to the emotions of others. Being skilled at doing so is often referred to as emotional intelligence. So, as we try to work our way out of a life governed by negative thoughts and self-talk, part of what we are doing is learning to develop our emotional intelligence.

Awareness

Emotional intelligence begins with an awareness of our own emotional states. This has to be clear and completely understood. One exercise that you can engage in is to go back and write down each instance where you have a thought of any kind. It can be negative self-talk or positive self-talk. Every time you have a thought that is worth writing down in your journal, also write down the emotional state that you're feeling at the time that you have the thought. See if you can recognize exactly what emotion it is. Sometimes the emotions will be simple and raw. You could be feeling depressed or melancholy, or maybe you feel angry. At other times the emotions might be a little more sophisticated, and in the beginning, it might be hard to identify them. So, you might feel angry, but what is really behind the anger? As an example, perhaps you are feeling a bit of resentment. In that case, rather than saying that it's anger, I would say that the true emotion is resentment.

You should also look to practice awareness when you're interacting with other people. Sometimes it's difficult to accurately estimate the emotions that other people are feeling. We are all bound to make mistakes when trying to interpret the feelings of others. Now, I'm not suggesting that you go out and actually confront people. Keep it to yourself. But try observing people—not just what they say or do, see if you can develop your emotional intelligence by becoming more aware of the emotional states that they may be experiencing.

In the last chapter, we mentioned that perhaps someone is having a bad day and it comes across that they don't like you. This is a skill that can become useful if you develop it over time. In other words, by closely observing people's emotions, it will help you to correctly interpret situations, rather than put it all as blame on you.

One way that you can do this, in the beginning, is to observe how some people are interacting with others casually. For example, your boss might come into your office and appear grouchy, and in the past, you would have interpreted this as either: "I did something wrong," or "My boss just doesn't like me." But with a little bit of heightened awareness, you might be paying attention to your boss as they interact with others in the office, and you might see that they have the same demeanor on that day with pretty much everyone they interact with. If that's the case, then you might use your emotional intelligence to try to understand what they are feeling and what their emotional state is. This has practical implications. When you're able to get a better sense of the emotional states that others are experiencing, you will be able to respond in a more appropriate manner. In all cases, taking an attitude of tolerance and understanding is going to be helpful. Again, that doesn't mean that you let yourself be abused. You use your judgment to determine when it's appropriate to be tolerant and when it's not.

Regulating Your Emotions

One of the aspects of emotional intelligence that is routinely considered is being able to regulate your own emotional states. This is very important when it comes to people who are suffering from negative programming, and who have been engaging in negative self-talk, possibly for decades. Learning to regulate your emotions is going to be one of the most important steps that you take.

When you have negative emotional states, many times, people simply experienced them without thinking about them. Start changing this by recognizing when you feel upset, depressed, frustrated, or angry. When you start to feel an emotional state, identify it in your mind. Say to yourself something to the effect of: "I am feeling frustrated right now." One of the things that this does is it helps to connect the left brain and the right brain together. Often the emotions we experience are felt through the right brain. Your language centers—and some people even suggest your consciousness (although nobody has proof about that really)—reside in your left brain. Emotions also rise from the nonverbal lower centers of the brain. That is why we feel emotions without always knowing how to vocalize about them. So, by making a statement about our emotional state, we help to involve the higher centers of our consciousness in the experience. This will help us to recognize our emotional states more clearly. And possibly more important, this is going to help us to manage them.

Frustration and anger are only useful if we recognize our emotional state and then do something about the cause of these feelings. Simply experiencing these emotions and fuming is not a sign of emotional intelligence. Instead, taking control of them and then turning them into positive self-talk is going to help you make actual progress in your life. Let's say that you get angry with your husband, who will not communicate when he is upset about something. Instead of just getting angry, you can recognize the emotional state and understand why you're feeling angry and frustrated. So, for example, you could then resolve to communicate in a loving and understanding way and explain to him that it would be helpful if he would explain how he is feeling and what is making him upset, rather than clamming up.

Becoming Sensitive to Emotional Signals

As you become more self-aware about your own emotional states and begin learning how to regulate them, you are also going to be able to develop more skills that will help you become sensitive to the emotional signals that others are giving off. In fact, this is something that you can start practicing right away. Again, I don't suggest confronting people, especially if it's not a personal relationship. Just make the observations and file them away in your own mind. But you can go beyond that. In other words, what you can do is start taking action based on the signals that you're getting from other people. This will help you learn and improve your emotional intelligence as well. There are going to be times when you make mistakes; however, you're going to find that you begin to find out when you are correct in your interpretation. So, this is a situation where you will learn as you go.

Changing Your Emotional States

Another aspect of emotional intelligence is learning how to alter your emotional state. This is actually easier than it sounds. Why is this important? This is actually totally relevant to the issue of negative self-talk. What happens with people who are prone to negative self-talk is they let themselves dwell in negative emotional states. Often you are not even fully aware of the emotional state that you are in. You might let it linger and gain more energy.

In any case, what is going to happen when you are letting yourself dwell in negative emotional states? Inevitably, you are going to start engaging in negative self-talk. You are already prone to this already, and so when you are feeling bad, the negative self-talk is going to come on and come on strongly.

This suggests learning to control your emotional states. We have already discussed the first step in this process, which is awareness. So, you need to recognize when you are in any given emotional state and tell yourself about it. "I am feeling really frustrated right now." Then work to replace the negative emotional state with a positive emotional state, or at least a neutral emotional state. One way to do this is to seek out an attitude of calm and peacefulness. Try breathing deeply and slowly. If you are able to, close your eyes as you breathe in and out, slowly. Don't think about anything. If you need to visualize something in order to keep your mind from engaging in negative self-talk, see yourself at the beach, or in an open field of flowers. Then, in your mind's ear, hear the sound of the waves lapping against the shore, or winds passing through some nearby trees. Keep breathing until you feel calm and relaxed.

If necessary, and if you have the ability to do so, go outside and take a quick five-minute walk. This can often help switch gears so that the negative emotional state that we have been experiencing gets replaced by more positive feelings.

You can also engage in positive affirmations when you recognize that you are feeling a negative emotional state. This can directly attack the tendency of your mind to bring out negative self-talk when you feel these types of emotional states.

Chapter 8: Strengthen the Mental Muscle

Now we've learned some ways that we can start transforming negative thoughts and emotions into positive ones. But remember that things are always going to get tough from time to time, and you are going to have to rely on yourself when times get difficult. You are your own best advocate and friend. Learn to rely on yourself first. This will help you get through tough situations, and it's also going to help you be a better partner, friend, and parent.

Get Tough and Have Your Own Back

If you have had negative self-talk throughout your life, then you are probably not a dominant person. And I am not going to suggest here that you become a dominant or controlling person, but what I am suggesting is that you learn to stand up for yourself. We all have our family, friends, and maybe you have a partner, but in the end, you have to stand up for yourself and not depend on others. Developing an ability to get tough in this manner is not just going to help you. It is also going to help you be a better person for others to have a relationship with, because they are going to be able to count on you when times get tough.

One of the first steps that you need to take when having your own back is not being afraid to speak out. Learn to speak out clearly and confidently and let people know that they cannot take you for granted. You should be able to express your needs clearly to other people and do it in a way that isn't hurtful.

Sometimes you are going to need to speak up. You might be treated unfairly at work, or you might get in a legal dispute with someone when you are in the right.

Don't be afraid to ask questions. Always make sure that people are communicating clearly and that you totally understand the situation. This is important in your personal and professional relationships. If you are having trouble with a manager at work, don't be afraid to take the initiative and go see them rather than wait for them to come and see you—or worse—they reprimand or fire you. Speak to them in a respectful but confident manner and ask questions. By asking questions, you can let your manager know that you are seeking to clarify the situation and get their expectations of you out in the open and crystal clear.

You should do the same when you are having conflicts in interpersonal relationships, and you don't know where the other person stands. You can take control by being the first person in the relationship to take action; you have your own back when you are the one to initiate communication and ask questions to get everything on the table.

Another aspect of having your own back is not relying strictly on what people say. Always verify what they claim in their speech by observing that they follow through with their actions. If someone owes you money, and they continually promise to pay you back, but they make no effort to do so, then you know this is a situation that you are going to need to take more seriously.

Boundaries are also important. All of us have some personal boundaries that we need to keep up, even with the people who are closest to us. If someone is violating what you feel are your personal boundaries, start by clearly explaining to that person what those personal boundaries are. If they continue to violate the boundaries after that, then you might reconsider your relationship with that person. If it's a family member, and you find that they are not respecting your personal boundaries even after you have clearly communicated them and what your expectations are, then you need to put some distance between yourself and that person until they make it clear that they are willing to respect the boundaries that you have set.

Remaining Strong in the Face of Adversity

As I said earlier, it is easy to write down thoughts in a book; it is hard to stay strong when times get tough. In order to remain strong, the first thing that you should do is adopt an attitude of calm acceptance. That doesn't mean that you're going to stay in a bad situation, rather, it means that you're going to be calm and peaceful and not get riled up with negative emotions that lead to panic and bring back the negative self-talk. From here, you should clearly work out the steps that you are going to take to change the situation. Use positive affirmations to give yourself the confidence to remain strong and positive. Keep asking questions—and look for the answers to develop steps to improve your situation.

Tips for Maintaining a Strong Mindset and Staying Positive

When faced with adversity, giving in to the same old negative thought processes is the easy way out, but it's also the natural inclination that you will have if you are coming from that place. Don't try to suppress your negative emotions—experience them as they are but use them to transform the situation. See a situation of adversity as a challenge, rather than viewing it as a negative. This will help you to start viewing life in an entirely different way. When facing a challenge, we try to work through it and get past it rather than giving in to it and feeling helpless. So, sit down and develop a plan to change the situation that is causing you adversity. Without a plan, the same problem is going to be there a week from now, a month from now, or a year from now. You are the one who has to take action to get out of the situation.

When faced with adversity, it is going to require you to call upon strength that you didn't realize you had. Break down the problem into small steps so that it's easier to force yourself to take the steps that are necessary in order to get out of it. Always use that approach when solving problems. View the problem, not as a whole, which is often overwhelming, but as smaller problems, each of which can be solved individually. Then start taking those small steps and making progress. You will find that you begin to develop a more positive attitude when using this type of approach, and you will also begin to feel better and gain confidence. Your emotional state will change from one that might be characterized as panic, to a serene calm, which gives you the confidence to push through.

Although it sounds strange, when you are feeling the most adversity, practice gratitude. Being thankful for the strength and abilities that you have will help you get through the most difficult times. There is no doubt that you have things to be thankful for, even in your darkest moments. By expressing gratitude, you are going to improve your mood and thought processes. This, in turn, is going to help you think more clearly and take a more positive attitude that is more conducive to solving your problems.

Also, focus on the positive. Remember filtering—there are always shades of gray in each situation that you encounter. Even if you are in an adverse situation where the negatives outweigh the positives—in the given moment—there are always positives to focus on and keep you upbeat.

Chapter 9: 500 Affirmations for a Positive and Optimistic Outlook

1. *I am unique, and my life has value.*
2. *I am confident.*
3. *I trust my own judgment.*
4. *I am optimistic and look forward to each day.*
5. *I am someone others can count on.*
6. *I choose to be successful.*
7. *I choose to be happy.*
8. *I love challenges; they bring out my strength.*
9. *I can create the life that I want.*
10. *I can draw on my own strength and power.*
11. *I believe in myself.*
12. *In the end, things work out for the best.*
13. *I accept myself for who I am.*
14. *It is human to make mistakes. I learn from my mistakes and move ahead stronger.*
15. *I feel good about being alive, and I enjoy my life.*

16. *Sometimes life is challenging, but it is also fun and rewarding.*
17. *Every problem presents an opportunity for growth.*
18. *I don't have to do anything; I choose to do things that work for me.*
19. *I can be counted on by others to meet any challenge.*
20. *I have the strength and stamina to get through anything.*
21. *I have compassion for myself and recognize that if I make a mistake it's not the end of the world.*
22. *I choose to be calm and peaceful.*
23. *I am successful.*
24. *With each passing day, I become more successful.*
25. *I can change the way I feel.*
26. *I recognize my strengths.*
27. *I attract people who are optimistic, happy, and positive.*
28. *I let go of negative thoughts and feelings.*
29. *I am honest and trustworthy.*
30. *I am capable of living a rich and full life.*
31. *I can have a fulfilling career.*
32. *My days are full of joy and laughter.*
33. *The number one emotion I feel is happiness.*
34. *I recognize the contributions of others but also of myself.*
35. *I will take credit when I deserve it.*
36. *I will not blame others for my mistakes but instead, take responsibility for them.*
37. *I make friends easily because I bring joy to people's lives.*
38. *I am pleasant to be around.*
39. *I am friendly and outgoing.*
40. *I have lots of energy and am passionate about everything that I do.*
41. *Amazing opportunities are there for me to take.*
42. *I will do what it takes to turn any wrong into a right.*
43. *I am not complacent; I have energy and enthusiasm for even the smallest task.*

44. *I have a lot to offer.*
45. *I can help people with my kindness and wisdom.*
46. *I look forward to meeting new people.*
47. *I find new situations and challenges exciting.*
48. *I have compassion and care for others with empathy and kindness.*
49. *I enjoy my work and consider no task to be beneath me.*
50. *I am smart and can tackle any problem.*
51. *I deserve love and happiness.*
52. *My thoughts and behavior are consistent.*
53. *I respect myself, and I respect others when they have earned it.*
54. *I deserve to be treated with respect and accept nothing less.*
55. *I am good to myself.*
56. *I know I can achieve anything I set my mind to.*
57. *Respecting myself first will help others respect me.*
58. *I like myself.*
59. *I can make my own decisions.*
60. *I have the power to create change.*
61. *I am happy with who I am, but I am willing to grow and change.*
62. *I let go of negative feelings about myself.*
63. *My self-discipline is growing stronger.*
64. *I am persistent and will work hard toward any goal.*
65. *I can choose any career path I want to.*
66. *I deserve to have a family that loves and respects me.*
67. *I am someone others can count on in a crisis.*
68. *I have the power to change myself.*
69. *I speak with clarity, confidence, and strength.*
70. *Other people value what I have to say.*
71. *My opinions matter.*
72. *If I have done my best, that is all I can do.*
73. *I have good self-esteem.*
74. *I love myself unconditionally.*

75. *I can heal myself.*
76. *I am willing and able to pay the price required to grow and become stronger.*
77. *If someone offers constructive criticism, it doesn't get me down.*
78. *Others respect me because I respect myself first.*
79. *Others love me because I love myself first.*
80. *Feeling confident comes naturally to me.*
81. *I can achieve anything and will do what it takes.*
82. *I have the power to change myself.*
83. *I do my best when meeting every challenge.*
84. *I have the power to change my situation.*
85. *I am flexible and open to change.*
86. *I forgive myself for making mistakes.*
87. *I can choose to live how I want to live.*
88. *I will not let others determine how I feel.*
89. *I choose to be happy no matter how bad things get.*
90. *Tomorrow is a new day with new opportunities.*
91. *I make mistakes, but everyone makes mistakes, and I learn from them.*
92. *I always look for the good in other people.*
93. *I am self-reliant and strong.*
94. *I am creative and see a way forward.*
95. *I attract positive and happy people.*
96. *I make other people happy because I am always striving to be happy and joyful.*
97. *I am eliminating negative energy from my life.*
98. *My talents make me unique.*
99. *I love and accept myself for who I am.*
100. *I am persistent and strive to look for solutions.*
101. *The universe fills me with joy and love.*
102. *People value my insight and knowledge.*
103. *I am always loved and respected.*
104. *I am not a prisoner of the past. I recognize mistakes I have made and learn from them, rather than dwelling on it.*

105. *I am full of courage and strength.*
106. *The universe is filling me with happiness, joy, and peace.*

Affirmations about Appearance

107. *I am not perfect, but nobody is.*
108. *I am beautiful and radiant.*
109. *Others see my beauty and are drawn to it.*
110. *I am always becoming more beautiful.*
111. *I accept who I am and appreciate my natural beauty.*
112. *I am attractive.*
113. *I am fit and healthy.*
114. *I am working to become even more fit, attractive, and healthy.*
115. *I take good care of my body.*
116. *I get the rest that my body needs and deserves.*
117. *I am losing weight and will lose weight as long as necessary.*
118. *My skin is smooth, radiant, and silky.*
119. *I have a wonderful smile.*
120. *I am not ashamed of my body.*
121. *My skin is unblemished.*
122. *I radiate an inner self-confidence, that enhances my natural beauty.*
123. *My hair is shiny, smooth, full, and beautiful.*
124. *I look great in pictures.*
125. *My smile makes others happy.*
126. *I attract people I want to attract.*
127. *Society cannot tell me what I am supposed to look like.*
128. *I will not give in to weight shaming; I lose weight to become healthier.*
129. *My body is beautiful.*
130. *I feel happy inside my body.*
131. *I feel healthy.*
132. *I will nourish my body with good and positive energy.*

133. *My happy and healthy attitude is making my body healthier every day.*
134. *I am sexy and desirable.*
135. *I nourish my body with the healthy foods and nutrients that it needs.*
136. *My teeth are white and beautiful.*
137. *My eyes sparkle when I smile.*
138. *My body is free of aches and pains.*
139. *My body is full of energy and can meet any challenge.*
140. *I am happy with my body the way it is.*
141. *I only eat when I am hungry.*
142. *When I am full, I stop eating.*
143. *I will do what's necessary to be healthy, but will not abuse my body.*
144. *My body is a temple, and I treat it as such.*
145. *If I am overweight, this has no impact on my worth or self-esteem.*
146. *If I am overweight, I will do what it takes to achieve optimal health.*
147. *Because I accept myself, I am comfortable in my own skin.*
148. *I dress appropriately for my body and look stylish and beautiful.*
149. *I am grateful for the food and nourishment the universe has provided me.*
150. *I am happy that I live in a world of plenty where I never want for food or nourishment.*
151. *I love exercising. It makes me feel great.*
152. *I am in control of my eating, and only eat as much as I need.*
153. *I am in control of my eating, and only eat foods that are healthy and nutritious.*
154. *I let go of any guilt I feel about food.*
155. *I am a real person and will not compare myself to Hollywood stars or models.*

156. *I am not embarrassed by my physical appearance.*
157. *I am attractive just the way I am.*
158. *I have a healthy relationship with food.*
159. *I can enjoy sweets and dessert once in a while without guilt or shame.*
160. *I am not ashamed of my body.*
161. *I will enjoy a life of health and longevity.*
162. *When I wake up in the morning, I feel strong, rested, and healthy.*
163. *My partner finds me attractive.*
164. *I am special.*
165. *My body does not define who I am.*
166. *I radiate inner and outer beauty.*
167. *My body image is not going to control my life.*
168. *I don't care what others think about my body or appearance.*
169. *I surround myself with love and acceptance.*
170. *I am secure in who I am, but always strive to improve.*
171. *I feel good about myself and my looks.*
172. *I do not need the validation of others for my appearance.*
173. *Nobody can reach perfection, but I can improve each day.*
174. *My kindness enhances my natural beauty.*
175. *My face is smooth and free of acne and blemishes.*
176. *I can feel my scars healing, and my skin becoming shiny and beautiful.*
177. *I look beautiful and also friendly; this makes it easy for others to approach me.*
178. *I feel good about the way I am without needing the validation of other people.*
179. *I do not compare myself to others. Everyone is unique and has their own values.*
180. *I seek to lose weight for my own health and well-being, not to please others.*

181. *Other people must accept me for who I am.*
182. *I cannot control what others think about my appearance.*
183. *I accept slow and steady progress when reaching my goals with exercise and healthy eating.*
184. *I enjoy eating a healthy diet.*
185. *I release all negative thoughts about my body.*
186. *I will not be shamed because of my appearance.*
187. *I can go in public without caring what others think about how I look.*
188. *I am OK if I eat an unhealthy meal or miss a day of exercise. We all deserve time to relax.*
189. *I eat to live and provide my body nourishment.*
190. *I do not feel guilty about eating.*
191. *I can control when I eat.*
192. *I feel great because I look great.*
193. *I look great no matter what I am wearing.*
194. *I feel great when I exercise and am full of strength and energy.*
195. *My strength and vitality grow every single day.*
196. *If I have a partner, they love me for who I am. My outer beauty is a bonus; it does not define me as a person.*
197. *I fill people's hearts with desire.*
198. *I am toned, fit, and strong.*
199. *I love the way I look when I see myself in the mirror.*
200. *I love how I look when I see myself in a photograph.*

Affirmations for Work and Career

201. *I work well under pressure.*
202. *I choose the kind of work I will do.*
203. *I have unlimited power to choose my career.*
204. *I am capable and will do what it takes to get ahead.*
205. *I have the knowledge necessary to make good decisions.*
206. *I make mistakes on the job, but I learn from them and do better next time.*

207. *People enjoy working with me and having me on their team.*
208. *I have the strength to overcome any obstacle.*
209. *I speak confidently at work.*
210. *I will be heard by my colleagues and supervisors.*
211. *I will not accept abuse and mistreatment at work.*
212. *My self-confidence is growing.*
213. *Today is going to be a great day at the office.*
214. *My colleagues at work love and respect me.*
215. *My opinion is valued by others.*
216. *My opinion is important.*
217. *I am intelligent and capable.*
218. *I can speak out with confidence, whether in a meeting or in private.*
219. *I am letting go of beliefs that restrict my success.*
220. *I deserve to get paid a fair wage for the work I do.*
221. *The world is full of unlimited opportunities.*
222. *I am capable of being my own boss.*
223. *I can start a business and become rich.*
224. *I set goals that I can meet.*
225. *My coworkers are supportive and friendly.*
226. *I have the power to attract wealth and prosperity.*
227. *I will let go of negative thoughts and emotions about others I work with.*
228. *I accept others for who they are and realize nobody is perfect.*
229. *I see the good in any situation at work.*
230. *I am smart enough to pursue any career that interests me.*
231. *I am focused on my goals and making progress.*
232. *I am always ready to accept new challenges.*
233. *I feel strong, confident, and able to meet any challenge I will face today.*
234. *I am enthusiastic about my work.*

235. *I will give my all to any task, no matter how small or trivial.*
236. *I will never stop growing.*
237. *During meetings, I feel strong and confident. My opinions matter.*
238. *Every day my confidence is increasing.*
239. *I am learning new things all the time and becoming more valuable to others.*
240. *I am grateful for the success I have achieved, and the coming years are only going to be better.*
241. *I am passionate about my work, and I look forward to each and every single day.*
242. *When I fail, it's a temporary setback, and I turn every failure into a success.*
243. *Failure is a learning opportunity.*
244. *I am surrounded by people who believe in me.*
245. *I look forward to going to work every single day.*
246. *I will push myself to become better.*
247. *I welcome any challenge and feel strong and confident.*
248. *The contributions I am making are powerful and valuable.*
249. *I am willing to work with anyone who respects me.*
250. *I deserve respect at work.*
251. *I am not afraid of change, and if I am not getting what I want at work, I will go elsewhere.*
252. *I have the confidence to change my situation if I need to.*
253. *I am growing all the time and becoming a better and stronger person.*
254. *I am free of self-doubt.*
255. *If I am disrespected, I have no fear of directly confronting it.*
256. *I am able to set goals at work and meet them in a timely fashion.*
257. *My potential for growth and achievement is limitless.*
258. *I succeed in everything that I do.*

259. *I am not afraid to strike out on my own.*
260. *I can succeed no matter what I do.*
261. *I am not afraid to pursue more education to make myself stronger and more useful to others.*
262. *I will mentor others who are like me, and teaching others makes me stronger.*
263. *I feel happy and free to make my own decisions.*
264. *I love my job but am not held prisoner by it.*

Affirmations for Wealth and Prosperity

265. *Wealth and prosperity flow to me daily.*
266. *I am able to manifest all the money that I need.*
267. *I am paying off all of my debts.*
268. *With each day that passes, I am becoming more financially secure.*
269. *The universe is full of wealth and abundance.*
270. *Money is never a problem for me.*
271. *I can make as much money as I need to be secure.*
272. *I feel good about money and prosperity.*
273. *Everyone deserves wealth, abundance, and prosperity.*
274. *Wealth and prosperity are flowing toward me.*
275. *I choose to be wealthy.*
276. *I enjoy my prosperity.*
277. *Being wealthy enables me to help others.*
278. *Making money is good for me, and helps me live independently.*
279. *I will not be a financial burden on others.*
280. *I am destined to make a lot of money.*
281. *Each year going forward, I will make more money than the last.*
282. *I always have enough money to meet my needs.*
283. *I always see new opportunities to make money.*
284. *My prosperity is always growing.*
285. *Wealth seems to find its way into my life.*
286. *My income is growing and will continue to grow.*

287. *I let go of a poverty mindset.*
288. *I am thankful for all the money I have received, and I look forward to receiving more money.*
289. *I love money and love sharing it with others.*
290. *Sharing my prosperity is a gift, not a burden.*
291. *I am gaining wealth through honest work.*
292. *I deserve to be wealthy, healthy, and prosperous.*
293. *I deserve my success.*
294. *I am a wealthy person.*
295. *I can create as much wealth as I want.*
296. *The world is full of opportunities to make money.*
297. *Wealth is a gift from the universe, and we all deserve it. But it is up to me to seize it.*
298. *Money makes me feel joyful, but my life does not revolve around money.*
299. *Money is good because it allows me to take care of myself and my family.*
300. *Every single day brings new opportunities to make money.*
301. *I am suddenly seeing new ways to make more money.*
302. *If I am not wealthy, I cannot help others.*
303. *The universe provides me with enough money to meet my needs.*
304. *There is wealth all around us; we only need to look for it.*
305. *I choose to think in terms of prosperity and wealth.*
306. *I let go of all the negative feelings I've had about money.*
307. *I am successful and prosperous.*
308. *I deserve to make a lot of money for what I do for others.*
309. *Prosperity flows to me without resistance.*
310. *I freely attract money and wealth.*
311. *I love money, but it's not the only good thing in my life.*

312. *I share money with others freely, because I know there are unlimited amounts of it.*
313. *I find it easy to make any amount of money.*
314. *I think in terms of prosperity and abundance.*
315. *I feel abundance all around me.*
316. *I attract others who can make money.*
317. *I am always thinking of new ways to make money and freely share my ideas with others.*
318. *I feel happy and joyful, and this attracts wealth, prosperity, and abundance.*
319. *Money is my birthright.*
320. *I deserve abundance and happiness.*
321. *I have the power to be successful and make any amount of money I choose.*
322. *I feel relaxed around money.*
323. *My debts are evaporating and being replaced by prosperity.*
324. *I can manage my finances with skill and confidence.*
325. *The amount of wealth in the universe is unlimited.*
326. *I do not feel guilty about my desire to be wealthy.*
327. *Wealth is not a matter of luck; I create wealth by applying the power of my mind.*
328. *When I create a business, it attracts customers eager to give me their money.*
329. *My customers give me their money because I provide them value in return.*
330. *The value I provide for others is worth unlimited amounts of money.*
331. *I can achieve any level of success.*
332. *I am extremely powerful and capable of earning money.*
333. *My financial situation improves with each passing day.*
334. *If I am not happy with my job, I am confident enough to find a new one that pays more money.*
335. *Each day, I feel more comfortable around money.*
336. *I am constantly attracting money into my life.*

337. *I am constantly attracting financial opportunities into my life.*
338. *People who can make money are attracted to me.*
339. *I will partner with others to make money, but I can take care of myself.*
340. *I do not need anyone to make enough money to take care of me, as I can support myself financially.*
341. *I find making money fun and enjoyable.*
342. *I feel confident that the universe will bring me all the money, wealth, and abundance that I could ever need.*
343. *My basic needs—food, shelter, and security—are always satisfied because I have enough money.*
344. *I have no problems accessing credit.*
345. *I have good credit, and it is always improving.*
346. *I feel comfortable being wealthy and having a lot of money.*
347. *I deserve to have more money than I ever dreamed of.*
348. *Poverty is evil; being rich is good.*
349. *I reject self-limiting beliefs that trap people in poverty or struggle.*
350. *I am smart enough to learn about business and finances.*
351. *I am a skilled investor who always seems to make money.*
352. *I can make money no matter how the economy is doing.*
353. *When I encounter struggles making money, I can come up with new plans to make new money.*
354. *There is always money to be made, and I will make it.*
355. *Everyone deserves to make money, but it is up to each of us to seek it out.*
356. *I will live a good and positive life, no matter how much money I make.*
357. *I will help others with my money, but won't sacrifice my wants and needs to do so.*
358. *If I am in a difficult situation, I will change it so that I can make more money.*

359. *The fact that others have made money proves I can make money too.*
360. *There are no limits to my financial success.*
361. *The more money I make, the more abundance flows to me.*
362. *My thoughts seem to attract money and wealth.*
363. *My bank account and stocks are constantly growing in value.*
364. *I never have problems paying any bills.*

Affirmations for Health and Safety

365. *I feel healthy and strong.*
366. *Every day, I feel youthful and vigorous.*
367. *I recover from illnesses easily.*
368. *I don't get sick often.*
369. *My body and immune system are strong.*
370. *I provide my body with the rest it needs to be healthy and strong.*
371. *I provide my body with the nutrients it needs for health.*
372. *I will live a long and prosperous life.*
373. *My body is free from disease and sickness.*
374. *Every day I become stronger.*
375. *My energy always seems to be increasing.*
376. *I feel younger than I did twenty years ago.*
377. *I will not abuse my body with alcohol or drugs.*
378. *I only eat healthy foods.*
379. *I enjoy exercise and the feelings of strength and health that it brings.*
380. *I will live a long time and will be free of disease.*
381. *My body is freeing itself from disease and disability.*
382. *I no longer feel any pain.*
383. *I am strong and flexible.*
384. *I can defeat cancer, heart disease, and diabetes.*
385. *I never seem to get sick, even when others around me are getting illnesses.*

386. I deserve to be completely free from illness.
387. I am free from back and joint pain.
388. I will not suffer from arthritis.
389. Every cell in my body is full of loving energy and is healthy.
390. If I am sick, I will return to health with time.
391. I will not let my mind get in the way of healing.
392. My body is grateful for the way I am taking care of it.
393. I am improving my health daily.
394. I enjoy the food that keeps my body healthy.
395. I live a life of balance, and this improves my health.
396. I am thankful for the health that I have enjoyed.
397. I am grateful for the gift of my life and pledge to live it to the fullest from this day forward.
398. I will seek out help with my health when I need it.
399. I respect my body and treat it with the respect it deserves.
400. I accept natural healing and welcome its power.
401. I deserve good health, and I claim it as my divine right.
402. Every day I am getting healthier.
403. I can enjoy junk food without guilt, but only in moderation.
404. I am in possession of a healthy mind.
405. I reject unnecessary worry about health. I will not be a hypochondriac.
406. I am safe.
407. I feel safe in my home.
408. I live in a good and safe neighborhood.
409. I deserve to be safe and protected.
410. I deserve safety and claim it as my divine right.
411. I trust my intuition and will listen to it if it warns me about my safety.
412. I feel safe wherever I go.
413. The universe protects me anywhere and at any time.
414. I am safe in this world.

415. *I feel safe no matter where I go. It feels like someone is watching out for me.*
416. *I have everything I need to be safe and secure.*
417. *I have friends and family I can depend on for safety.*
418. *The world is full of kindness.*
419. *I have the power to create my own safety and security.*
420. *My loved ones are always safe and secure.*
421. *My children are safe and protected.*
422. *My body is safe and without risk.*
423. *I am safe at all times.*
424. *I feel secure when I travel.*
425. *I am always protected.*
426. *Everyone I love is safe and secure.*
427. *I am free from accidents and danger on the road.*
428. *I am always safe when I fly on an airplane.*
429. *My home is a haven of safety, protected from everything in this world.*
430. *I am safe and protected by the universal good. My world is surrounded by kindness and joy.*
431. *I am confident in my ability to protect myself and those around me.*
432. *My body is safe, secure, and protected.*
433. *I choose to feel safe and secure.*
434. *I feel safe and protected at all times.*
435. *I feel protected by the kindly divine spirit.*
436. *My intuition warns me of any potential danger.*
437. *I see myself traveling home at night in safety and security.*
438. *My world is a safe world.*
439. *My family is always safe.*
440. *I will take action to enhance the safety and security of my home.*

Affirmations for Love and Romance

441. *I deserve a loving relationship.*

442. I deserve the respect of my partner.
443. I will only stay in a relationship based on loving kindness and respect.
444. I refuse to be abused or taken advantage of.
445. I will make my needs and feelings known to my partner.
446. I am confident about expressing my needs.
447. I love, admire, and respect my partner, and expect love, admiration, and respect in return.
448. I have unconditional love for my partner.
449. I deserve unconditional love.
450. I accept my partner for who they are, and expect them to accept me for who I am.
451. I expect my personal boundaries to be respected.
452. I will not stay in a relationship that is physically or emotionally abusive.
453. I am strong and confident and deserve unconditional love and respect.
454. I will respect the personal boundaries of others.
455. I will not force my partner to change and accept them for who they are.
456. I will not judge the people in my life, and they will not judge me.
457. I enjoy spending time with the people that I love.
458. I feel fulfillment in my relationships.
459. I am in a relationship where I am constantly growing and becoming whole.
460. I show my loved ones, including my partner, that I care about them.
461. I love unconditionally even though the people around me might not always treat me with respect.
462. I will show my loved ones how much I care for them.
463. I attract loving people into my life.
464. I am not afraid of change and will change my relationships if necessary.

465. *I am able to communicate openly and honestly with my partner, friends, and family.*
466. *I am confident enough to communicate with complete honesty.*
467. *I do my best not to hurt the feelings of others in my life.*
468. *I do not fear emotional intimacy—I embrace it.*
469. *I welcome the love that the universe brings me.*
470. *I feel joy and loved when around my partner.*
471. *I am letting go of anger and negative feelings when thinking about my partner.*
472. *I reject feelings of jealousy and resentment.*
473. *I feel a sense of contentment when surrounded by the people I love.*
474. *My partner makes me feel safe and secure.*
475. *If I don't have a partner, it is only a matter of time before I find the perfect mate.*
476. *There is love and joy throughout the universe, and I will find someone to share it with.*
477. *I have unlimited love to give and share with others.*
478. *I love my family and accept them unconditionally.*
479. *I will share unconditional love with a partner.*
480. *When I get in petty disputes with loved ones, I forgive and forget and move on.*
481. *I will take responsibility when I hurt other people's feelings.*
482. *When I have injured another person emotionally, I will heal them.*
483. *While I will freely give of myself, I will expect to be paid back in like with kindness, love, and joy.*
484. *I deserve healthy and happy relationships.*
485. *I deserve unconditional love.*
486. *I deserve to have my own family.*
487. *I deserve love and respect.*
488. *My family provides love, care, and security.*
489. *I experience joy when I see my loved ones.*

490. I know that my partner has my back at all times.
491. I am strong enough to provide complete support for my partner.
492. I enjoy celebrations with my family members.
493. I enjoy getting together with friends.
494. My friends can count on me, and I can count on them.
495. I have many friends who will provide support when I need it.
496. I am strong and able to give my friends support when they need me.
497. Life is full of joy, friendship, and love.
498. I look forward to each day, and the joy and love I will experience.
499. I am a wonderful and supportive parent and support my children with unconditional love.
500. I am strong, capable, kind, and loving, and would make a perfect partner for anyone.

Conclusion

Thank you for taking the time to read *Self Talk: The Ultimate Guide to Transforming Negative Thinking into Positive Thinking and Skyrocketing Self-Esteem, Confidence, Productivity, and Mental Toughness, Including 500 Daily Affirmations.*

I truly hope that you have found this book to be helpful and that you will find it useful in going forward. If you have enjoyed the book and found it to be educational, please leave a review on Amazon, I would much appreciate it.

The words that we say inside our heads throughout the day, every single day, have a large influence over how we feel about ourselves. The types of thoughts echoed by our inner voice are effectively running on autopilot, and are guided by programs that have wired our mind to think with certain negative patterns. The groundwork for these programs was laid down long ago, starting in childhood. It may seem that it is impossible to overcome them; however, we can learn to reprogram our "autopilot" and replace the negative self-talk we hear every day with positive thoughts and feelings. These, in turn, will lead to better and healthier results throughout our entire lives.

I hope that the methods discussed in this book will help you and that you will have stories of a positive transformation to share. I look forward to hearing them and will enjoy reading about them.

Thank you again for taking the time to read this book! May your life be filled with many happy and joyous days in the years ahead.

Check out another book by Mark Dudley

www.ingramcontent.com/pod-product-compliance
Lightning Source LLC
Chambersburg PA
CBHW070046230426
43661CB00005B/778